To Elly Laderborg,
  — whose devotion and capable leadership has so greatly contributed to the quality and spirit of the choral and other musical groups of CLBS during this past year, this book is a small token and expression of my personal appreciation.

Edwin W. Petrusson

September 11, 1975

The
Church
Music
Handbook

The
Church Music Handbook

A handbook of practical procedures and suggestions

Lynn W. Thayer

Illustrations by ENRIQUE GARAY

ZONDERVAN PUBLISHING HOUSE
OF THE ZONDERVAN CORPORATION
GRAND RAPIDS, MICHIGAN 49506

THE CHURCH MUSIC HANDBOOK
© 1971 by Zondervan Publishing House
Grand Rapids, Michigan

Second printing 1974

Library of Congress Catalog Card Number 70-146584

All rights in this book are reserved

With those exceptions noted below, no part of this book may be used or reproduced in any manner whatsoever without written permission of the publisher or author except brief quotations embodied in critical reviews or articles. Forms, Charts, Blanks, Outlines may be used in toto or adapted for individual and local needs. For information address the publisher.

It would be quite impossible to list all who have assisted with this book. Several individuals, however, must be acknowledged for their valuable counsel, suggestions, and association:

Dr. Richard C. von Ende, Chairman, Division of Fine Arts, McMurry College, Abilene, Texas;

Dr. E. A. Thormodsgaard, formerly Head, Music Department, University of Texas at El Paso;

Dr. Ralph H. Seiler, pastor of the Travis Park United Methodist Church, San Antonio, Texas;

Dr. Olav E. Eidbo, Head, Music Department, U. T., El Paso;

Prof. Robert Stevenson, University of California at Los Angeles; and the Rev. John Whitney MacNeil, pastor of the First Congregational Church, Sarasota, Florida.

Profound appreciation is expressed to the University Research Institute of the University of Texas at El Paso for its material assistance in the preparation of this handbook.

Artist Enrique Garay is warmly commended for his interpretations of ideas depicted in line drawings and diagrams.

Printed in the United States of America

To my wife
CORA
*without whose love, companionship, and understanding
this book could not have been written*

"Much thought and a reservoir of long and valuable experience have gone into the concept and writing of this book. It should be a valuable contribution to the whole field of church music and *required reading for ministers, choir directors, and the church music committee.*
It is probably the most complete manual for the operation of the church music program that I have read."

Richard C. von Ende, Chairman
Division of Fine Arts
McMurry College, Abilene, Texas

"There is a warmth and personal feeling throughout that I have never felt in *any* other books. Contents — as I have said — are exactly what is needed!"

E. A. Thormodsgaard
Formerly Head, Music Department
University of Texas at El Paso

"A book of this nature would be extremely helpful to music directors throughout the churches of our country. Ministers, too, would gain tremendous insights from the reading of this book, as they are related to the music ministry of the local church. As you know, I have read a good many books dealing with the music ministry in the local church, but I must say that your book is by far more detailed, carefully thought through, and practical than any of the books that I have thus far read. You are dealing with the real issues as well as pointing in the direction that would help to create a more effective music ministry in the local church."

Ralph H. Seiler, Pastor
Travis Park United Methodist Church
San Antonio, Texas
Formerly District Superintendent
New Mexico United Methodist Conference

CONTENTS

Preface (For Whom This Book Was Written)
Introduction
Chapter 1. The Music Committee 19
    2. Areas of Representation 21
    3. Specific Duties of the Music Committee . . . 24
    4. Selecting Your Music Director 28
    5. The Director's Technique 35
    6. Qualifications of Your Organist 39
    7. Organist-Director? 45
    8. The Volunteer Choir 48
    9. The Adult Choir 61
    10. Age-Group Choirs 68
        The High School Choir 73
        The Junior High School Choir 78
        Fourth, Fifth, Sixth Grade Choir 79
        The Primary Choir 81
    11. Congregational Singing 83
    12. Assistance in the Church School 99
    13. Training Classes 101
    14. Special Services and Programs 105
    15. Massed Group Festivals and Competitions . . 110
    16. Vestments 120
    17. Your Music Room 126
    18. Equipment 142
    19. Your Music Library 148
    20. Your Instrumental Program 151
    21. Ethics, Personal Relationships 153
    22. Improving Music Facilities 158
    23. The Choir Rehearsal 164
    24. Budgeting 170
    25. Planning for the Future 172
    26. Maintaining Year-Round Interest 181
Appendix
    List of Texts, Training Materials, References . . . 186

FORMS, CHARTS, BLANKS, OUTLINES

Contract, music director	31
Requirements for the organist	41
The Ministry of Music	49
Application for choir membership, constitution, etc.	53
Duties of adult choir personnel	62
Ministry of Music	72
Church school music leaders	100
Services and programs, check sheet	107
Property check-out cards	108
Job assignment cards	109
Housing accommodations	111
Housing cards for individuals	112
Meal agreement	114
Choir robe inventory and use list	122
Proposed music quarters	138
Equipment needed	140
Music program requirements	159
Budget account form	171
Music resources survey	173
Suggestions for church music program	177
Applications for chancel and children's choirs	178
Indication of interest	179

FOR WHOM THIS BOOK WAS WRITTEN

Your Music Committee, a sincere group of laymen, needs to know how to set up and maintain the program of music in the worship of your church. They can learn here what the program can accomplish; what to expect, and what not to expect of members of the music staff. As pastors and music directors inevitably come and go, the church may learn from these pages how to preserve its music program in unbroken continuity.

The Session or Board Member held responsible for guidance of the entire music program will discover in what areas lay personnel can be called upon to implement the details which he cannot possibly find time to accomplish himself.

Your Pastor, whether he has a large church with a staff of assistants, or a small church where he, himself, must carry the full responsibility, will find here common sense answers to many of his questions concerning the music program he would like to have.

Your Director of Music who provides and instructs his music committee members with these outlines of projected duties and areas of responsibilities can begin to devote more time to the music itself instead of being bogged down with non-musical details which others can do just as well. He will at the same time "broaden the base" of participating personnel.

Your Organist can literally make or break your worship atmosphere from his/her position at the keyboard.

Your Congregation wants and deserves to know more about the music of their worship.

The College Church Music Instructor wishes to provide his students with a thoroughly tested "how to do it" manual, equally understandable to both lay and trained personnel. The line between musical and supporting activities is clearly drawn.

THE COLLEGE MUSIC STUDENT, who is preparing to be a leader in school, church, and community music often overlooks a most vital factor in true success: the ability to delegate appropriate responsibilities to others. We trust that in these pages suggestions may be found which will enable him to use his own resources to the best advantage and at the same time utilize the talents of his associates to the utmost.

* * * * *

The ideas in this handbook are both realistic and workable. There is not one paragraph of theory which has not been successfully applied many times.

It is my prayer that each of you who uses this outline may discover additional ways to make more soul-enriching the music of your worship of Almighty God.

To our Lord — only our best!

THE AUTHOR

INTRODUCTION

The responsibility for the music in your church may rest in the hands of a committee, or a single individual such as the pastor, or a member of the board or session. Regardless of your type of administration, the practical procedures described in this handbook can be of concrete value to you and to your fellow workers.

You proceed to hire a director or a minister of music and look forward with high expectations to congregational singing, choirs of all ages, and musical achievements that will rival those of the heavenly hosts! You agree completely with your leader when he tells you that all of you can be satisfied with nothing less than *"to our Lord — only our best!"*

You expect him to lead, to train, to advise, to understand, to work *musically* with all areas of the church. This he is quite ready to do if you will let him! "Let him?" you ask in amazement. "Yes, we are giving him freedom to work out his ideas in all departments!"

What else are you "letting" him do? Are you standing by and "letting" him struggle with all the non-musical details that attend such a program, and that consume so many minutes that those he has left for the music itself are precious few?

Your minister of music or director should be doing nothing that someone else in the congregation can do! This is especially true in the vast majority of our churches where this music leader is employed on a part-time basis. Such mechanical matters as checking on attendance, keeping records, setting up chairs, maintenance of the music library, most of the telephoning, and the host of other necessary details can, and *must* be done by lay personnel.

Only in this way can any church receive full value for the dollars it spends for the salaries of its leadership. Only with this help can the director prepare his music effectively each week, examine and choose good and appropriate music, plan with the pastor and execute the year-round program, and, most important of all, make the church's music the powerful force it can be in (1) helping to win souls to Christ, and (2) keeping them strong and steadfast in practical working faith. Fortunately today more and more pastors who have discovered this truth are taking the necessary steps to free the director of non-musical, but essential details of the program. They are seeing the results justify many times over the effort required to set up and maintain the mechanical assistance to the minister of music.

The pastor is not expected to dust the pews or mow the lawn. The music director should not have to put the rehearsal room in order or personally telephone choir members for an extra rehearsal.

As each new member joins the music committe or lay group of the department, his predecessor's copy of this outline should be passed on to him to be studied carefully and prayerfully in preparation for his job ahead. Frequent reference and reminder

will facilitate the discharge of specific duties throughout the year.

This handbook is not intended or presumed to be complete in all possible details or phases of church music program operation. It is hoped that the suggestions contained herein will in turn bring to mind additional ways in which you can assist your music director to do his job better.

The pastor and director who will utilize fully the lay personnel available will immediately see results which otherwise would be impossible. They will discover many additional ways in which more people can share duties and enhance the success of the program.

(It won't hurt a bit to have other members of the congregation read this either! Perhaps more of them will begin to appreciate what must go on behind the scenes to make possible the worshipful music they expect on Sunday morning. It won't harm them at all to discover that suitable, appropriate worship music doesn't just *happen*!)

The illusion still persists with many people that they are paying a choir director for two hours on Thursday night and one worship hour on Sunday. Few realize the hours of study and preparation required outside the hours of actual rehearsal to make the worship a smooth and integral whole.

Today the shoddy work of the director who spends *only* the Thursday night and Sunday hours on the music soon becomes apparent to everyone concerned. Then our churches plead with their colleges and universities to "send us someone who is *trained* in church music leadership!"

It is hoped that through these pages the layman may better understand what makes a church music program "tick" and just how he can aid in the mechanical aspects of the program.

One day the director leaves. Pastor and music committee are face to face with the formidable task of hiring his successor. To whom shall they turn? For just what shall they ask? Guidelines in several chapters are designed to help them shape the requirements for both directors and organists.

The Church Music Handbook

CHAPTER 1

THE MUSIC COMMITTEE

Administration of the music in most of our churches takes many forms. It has no accepted or set formula. It may be accomplished through (1) personal direction of the pastor; (2) delegation of most decisions to a single member of the "session" or board of the church; (3) a worship commission (certain members of the general board); (4) a music committee; or (5) a combination of the above. While several denominations outline areas of responsibility quite specifically, others are general in their recommendations.

Often the music committee meets periodically, or on call, to hear a report on "how things are going." Pros and cons may be discussed, suggestions made on what *should* be done, and then adjournment is called to end both the meeting and all serious thought on the part of the laymen until the next session. The director is left with more things to do than he had before the meeting! When the suggestions are not followed, he is often subject to censure for not getting them done. This procedure is inefficient and outdated.

In more fortunate circumstances the committee embraces a group of laymen who recognize the mechanical details incidental to a successful program and who themselves assume responsibility for accomplishing them. Each is assigned to a specific area. Each concentrates his efforts in this area; at the same time relating the progress in this field to the united success of the entire department.

Activities in each area are coordinated and guided by the director or minister of music. After major policies are established via conferences between pastor, director, and the music committee, the actual operational procedures should be placed in the hands of the director. His must be the decisions as to appropriate music, conduct of the rehearsals, and other means of accomplishing the ends agreed upon.

His liaison with the pastor will be constant and continuing, to assure that his direction is in keeping with the overall goals of the church and its central leadership. Pastor-director relationships are clearly portrayed by Lovelace and Rice in their book, *Music and Worship in the Church* (Abingdon Press).

When the major elements of the program are determined the director goes about the selection of his lay assistants. For each of the major activities he will attempt to select one person who has both a personal interest and the ability to get the job done.

One person who is definitely a "non-musician" is needed for every music committee. To those who like music, and to those whose background does not include music training we are equally responsible. This non-musical person helps us to keep our perspective from becoming lopsided in favor of music which might be effective only to one group of people.

Here is an excellent opportunity for "missionary work," by the way. Frequently the person who has been lukewarm—or less—to the whole music program is won over completely after a few months of service with the committee. He has a close look at music at work. He sees its power as a part of the act of worship. He becomes an enthusiastic booster for that of which he was only passively aware for so long a time, and quite often voluntarily takes on an active assignment in the program. Of course the director must then find another non-musician for the committee.

CHAPTER 2

AREAS OF REPRESENTATION

The fully-developed program of a large church obviously requires much more personnel than a beginning one, or than a complete one for a small church. The church with a new program or a limited one will select first from the areas listed in this chapter those which it can best develop with its current budget and available staff.

Choice of leadership has to come first, of course. The adult choir is the heart of the entire music program. It carries the first and main obligation for the music of the worship service. It is the group which brings new hymns to the congregation and provides leadership in all singing of hymns and responses. It helps to organize, to sponsor, encourage, and develop the younger groups who will soon become members of the adult organizations. Which additional choir(s) of young people will be added will depend on the numbers of each age available in the church parish. (See chapter on age-group choirs.)

>   Areas of a complete church music program
>   Choice of leadership
>   The adult choir

Age-group choirs
    High school
    Junior high school
    Intermediate
    Primary
Congregational singing
Music in the church school
The organ, pianos, and equipment
Training classes
    Song leaders
    Accompanists
    Music reading
Instrumental activities
    Orchestra
    Band
    Small ensembles

Your music director, pastor, and you on the committee will determine together where your emphasis will be placed as the total program grows. The training classes and instrumental groups usually follow when the remainder of the program is firmly established. The areas are listed, not in order of importance necessarily, but to outline desirable extent of the program and to show where lay help will be needed. In following chapters procedures are presented for planning and action in each of these areas.

How often we hear, "But our church is so small! Our problems are so different from those of a big church!" Many years of experience in churches of all sizes have convinced the writer that most of the main problems have the same basic roots, and that the *size* of the problem is largely determined by the size of the church.

CHURCH MUSIC PROGRAM
MUSIC DIRECTOR
MUSIC COMMITTEEMAN
MUSIC COMMITTEEMAN

CHAPTER 3

SPECIFIC DUTIES OF THE MUSIC COMMITTEE

Since the church music program begins usually in a modest way, with possibly only the adult choir, and grows with the addition of one age-group choir and then a second, this handbook deals first with the specific non-musical matters in which the individual members of the committee can relieve the director.

Factors pertinent to this growth are discussed for the benefit of new committee members, and for other laymen of the young church. Unfortunately, music directors sometimes change more frequently than the governing boards of the church. It is important, therefore, for the latter to know how to build and maintain a growing program. Loss of continuity which often results when a new choir leader is hired can be avoided when the supporting committee knows where, how, and why the program is going!

Policy-Making

In any program growth and expansion there gradually evolve certain desired methods of procedure. The music committee comes to learn what works well and what does not in this job of helping to make better and more effectual Christians. Through their firsthand knowledge of these procedures, the committee can intelligently advise and support the pastor in his tremendous responsibility of guiding the whole church.

Inevitably, in time, a new director must be employed. The accompanist has to be replaced. Who in the church is ready with an outline of definite qualifications which the new candidate must meet? How often has a church found to its dismay, and too late, that the new director was not qualified to carry on all the departments of their former program? What shall be the policies governing the use of the organ and other musical equipment?

The music committee that can accomplish the preliminary screening, present its recommendations to the board and the pastor, and assist in making final determinations is indeed a jewel of great price.

The latter part of the handbook deals with a number of more general policies which need to be considered by both the new and the experienced committee. (Parenthetically, the "staggered" method of replacement in which only one, or at most, two members are replaced each year is the best insurance for a successful continuing program.)

It is highly desirable that each member be persuaded to stay on long enough to help train his replacement on the committee.

The reading of Chapter 8, "The Volunteer Choir," is a "must" for every member of the committee and the governing board of the church.

Musical Procedures

A word of admonition here may be appropriate and may save many heartaches and disappointments. Let us assume that the general procedures, current policies, and the *general* types of music desired have been agreed upon between the new director and pastor and other members of his staff. The particular choice of music, the running of rehearsals, the selection and acceptance of choir members, and other matters primarily musical *must* be left to the decision of the director. This is the field for which he is trained. You are paying him. His must be the accountability for assembling and utilizing the details which in his judgment will be successful.

One does not tell the director what anthem he is going to use for this Sunday (except where dictated by denominational edict) any more than one tells the pastor just what he is going to say on his chosen subject. One does not tell the director how to run his rehearsal any more than one dictates to the pastor how he shall counsel the person who comes for spiritual help. On the other hand constructive suggestions brought in the privacy of a conference—not in the middle of an already planned practice—are welcomed and considered for possible use.

An autocratic "because I say so" is never good under any circumstance, of course. The considerate director shares with his choir the reasons for certain procedures. From them he often receives suggestions which may be beneficial to the whole program. He cannot, however, allow adopted standards to be pulled thither and yon by well-meaning but less-informed individuals. He must deal tactfully but firmly with ideas or thoughts which in his judgment might be inimical to the ultimate good of the group.

"Oh, let's not sing *this* anthem. I've never liked it!" "Truthfully, there are many others I like better, myself," he must be ready to reply, "but the choir is not just for you or for me, is it? It's for the whole congregation. Some folks seem to get much from it, and have asked for it again—so we're doing it for them."

Mutual respect and confidence in professional integrity must exist between pastor, music director, and committee. The pastor knows exactly what he wishes to accomplish in a complete worship service and it is the music director's duty to do his utmost to help in seeing that it is done. The pastor has an equal responsibility, however, to respect his colleague's professional ability and to consider suggestions which could add beauty and effectiveness.

Mutual discussion of problems at committee meetings may well influence the director to modify or change some courses of action adopted earlier. This can help also in the acceptance of new ideas or plans. The wise director is always alert to tailor the music program to the needs of his pastor and congregation. The intelligent pastor is at all times ready to try suggestions from those who are sincerely trying to "hold up his arms."

Musical Balance Wheel

The music committee is, perforce, the "balance wheel" of this department for the church. When those persons employed for leadership in singing or playing cannot or will not perform the functions mutually agreed upon at hiring time it is the duty of this particular church unit to support the pastor in replacement action. It is, therefore, imperative that the entire committee be thoroughly conversant with the aims and method of operation of the church music department.

CHAPTER 4

SELECTING YOUR MUSIC DIRECTOR

As surely as water rises no higher than its source, your program will be not one whit better than the person whom you employ to direct it! How do you go about securing just the right man or woman for the job? What guidelines shall you use? The following outline is not all-inclusive but it does set forth basic items which should not be overlooked:

The Music Director

PERSONAL

   Avowed and demonstrated life as a Christian
   Physical fitness
   Maturity in emotions and judgment
   Attractive personality
   Friendly attitude
   Ability to get along with people
   Personal philosophy of the place of music in worship
   Dependability
   Past and/or present church membership

PROFESSIONAL

   General educational background
   Professional training in music, general

Training in music of the church
Background and understanding of music of this denomination
Training and experience in successful leadership in
  (a) adult choirs
  (b) other age groups
Experience in organizing and directing a church-wide music program
Understanding of, and sympathy with local church and church school organizations, beliefs, and administration
Knowledge of this church's rituals and procedures
Practical knowledge of Christian Education
Knowledge of teaching procedures for all age groups
Willingness to cooperate in the purpose and plans of this church for children, youth, adults

* * * * *

As with the general ministry, the competent individual must be considered as worthy of his hire. While personal dedication should be expected, the church must be ready and willing to offer financial recompense for professional qualified services in keeping with its other departments of trained ministry. In some instances a complete new line of thinking in the church must come about before its people accept music ministry on the same programmed and budgeted basis as its central leadership.

This status of music ministry does not have to be defended. It now exists so successfully as a tremendous power in winning *and holding* men and women to Christian service in so many thousands of churches of this country that it testifies for itself. On the contrary, churches that have *not* developed a strong ministry in music find themselves in a position difficult to defend! Those who cannot or will not see the great force of this ministry about them continue to limp along on a catch-as-catch-can basis, losing scores of their young people annually, the lifeblood of Christ's continuing church!

Such items as three- to four-week trial periods and/or observation of the candidate in his present location of employment deserve consideration. The capable individual will not fear to "show his wares" for the church he knows to be serious and intent on a well-rounded program of spiritual service.

Contracts

Conservatively speaking, probably eighty-five percent of the misunderstanding and grief which arise between the central church administration and its music staff could be eliminated by use of written contracts outlining services to be rendered and concrete returns to be expected for them. How often have we heard, "When they hired me they told me the position included one night a week for choir rehearsal and one Sunday service. Now they expect me to be at church two or three nights a week, and for two worship services, with no change in pay!" or "Our music director objects strenuously if we ask him to lead the worship music in *one* extra midweek special service!"

Definite written agreements are especially required when the music personnel may be employed on a part-time basis. The church must keep in mind that such individuals must allocate the remainder of their hours to making up the remainder of their living, and be prepared to make adequate return for the time and energy used.

The following items are representative of those on which complete agreement is imperative:

>number of services
>choirs involved
>rehearsals for each
>conferences with pastor
>yearly planning
>extra meetings and music for them
>amount to be spent for music budget
>private teaching: time allowed
>use of church facilities
>expected participation in general church life
>remuneration for regular services
>additional pay for extra activities, if not included in yearly amount
>vacation period

Selecting Your Music Director

    advance notice which will be mutually acceptable if termination of service is desired

Each situation will have its own requirements, to be thoroughly discussed and mutually agreed upon *at the time of employment.* As a starter, something like the following might serve:

Contract

It is hereby agreed that _____ is to serve as music director of _____ church for the period of one year, beginning _____ 19___. Duties shall consist of preparing for, and directing the following:

1. One evening choir rehearsal of at least two hours, weekly, on a night mutually acceptable to choir, organist, and director
2. Music requirements: anthems, hymns, responses, for ___ Sunday worship service(s) weekly
3. One junior choir rehearsal of one hour, minimum, on Saturday mornings
4. Participation of junior choir in a regular worship service once each month
5. Whatever extra rehearsals may be required for special observance of Christmas and Easter
6. Preparation of music for, and participation in a maximum of six additional special services of worship during the year
7. Coordinating with the pastor on a monthly basis, at least one month in advance, the general and specific type of music and hymns to be used, in order that the worship service may be effectual and coherent, and that the choirs may be adequately prepared for such services.

For these services the director shall be paid a minimum of $_____ monthly for the year's period. Additional services for which the director's assistance may be required shall be reimbursed at the rate of $_____ per service.

It is further agreed that such mechanical details as the care, issuance, and collecting of music, telephoning for special rehearsals, care of robes, and other adjuncts to successful choir operation will be performed by church personnel under the supervision and direction of the director. The director is thus enabled to put his full efforts in the musical enhancement of the worship service.

It is further agreed that this covenant may be altered by mutual consent at any time during the year to fit the needs of a growing church.

Signed_____
(pastor)

_____
(music committee)

_____
(music director)

Whether the candidate is employed on either part- or fulltime basis does not matter. A complete understanding and acceptance of conditions by both parties can form the foundation of a pleasant and fruitful period of devoted service.

It should be made clear to all concerned from the beginning that the director holds final responsibility for the program and that ultimate decisions within the department must be his. This is especially important for the other members of the music staff to know, *e.g.* accompanists or assistants. The music committee cannot be namby-pamby and leave it up to the director himself to say, "I am the boss." The committee has the obligation to make clear to each newly added staff assistant his relationship to, and with the leader of the program.

Of all parts of this handbook, the above paragraphs will undoubtedly be the most frequently ignored! Churches that *will* take the time and effort to establish mutual acceptance, however, will find it to be the most profitable of insurance.

As the program grows, provisions of such contracts increase, of course, up to, and including full-time music ministry. The music committee will state what it sees to be the needs of the church's music program, and will be responsible for obtaining properly qualified personnel.

Such items as paid vacations, encouragement to professional growth through added study and attendance at church professional music conferences will warrant mutual exploration.

The music director becomes a "member of the family" as he rightfully participates in the long-range planning of the complete church program, and is recognized financially on a scale commensurate with pastor and other trained leaders. If he refuses to participate in such planning and recognition of his work in relation to the whole, it is time for the committee to find someone who will do so.

Pitfalls to Be Avoided

It seems only fair to point out to the committee certain situations which should be avoided. Occasionally someone who has had a measure of training in piano and/or voice will apply to a church for the position of choir director for the purpose of making a little "pin money." At other times unknowing church board or committee personnel have urged someone in the congregation with some general music training to "help us out by leading the choir!" A third type of undesirable situation may develop when the trained director is lost to another position and a member of the choir is prevailed upon to "lead us until we can find another director."

I hear a fervent chorus of "Amen's!" from the host of ministers who have weathered some of these ordeals, and who read over my shoulder as I caution church lay personnel to shun such relationships.

Unfortunately even an excellent background in general music is only the first of several requisites in the preparation for choir leadership. One good lady of my acquaintance stoutly declares, "I have studied music for twenty-five years. I *ought* to be able to lead a choir!" She proceeds to "carry" her choir through its anthems and hymns via the sheer strength of her own voice, without training them to do their anthems themselves. And some people in her church wonder why the choir does not grow, or improve, or "sound any better!"

Would you accept for your pulpit a man who maintains, "I have been talking for twenty-five years; I *ought* to be able to be a minister!"? Churches that would shudder at the thought of installing such a minister still limp along with whatever pseudo-music leader comes along. Fortunately the number of churches like this is rapidly dwindling.

Fruits of Leadership, Good and Bad

Boys and girls and young people of most of our high schools are today being exposed to much music of excellent quality extremely well performed. It is to the everlasting credit of our high school choral leaders that a substantial percentage of this music is in the "sacred" category, spiritual in nature, and suitable to be presented in worship of Almighty God.

Why are we not reaping the full benefit of this spiritual training of these youngtsers by providing skilled leadership in our churches where these singers may continue these inspiring experiences?

Should not their first and greatest spiritual thrills (and I use the term most carefully and reverently) come from experiences in their own churches? Can we honestly blame them for refusing to be identified with slipshod, haphazard products in the choir loft? Thousands of churches in the United States today are providing the inspired skilled leadership in their choirs that makes the carry-over of both high school and earlier age-group choir training into the adult singing on the church a smooth and effective process. You who wish to substantiate this statement will not have to go far to do so.

What kind of leadership are *you* furnishing for your youth?

CHAPTER 5

THE DIRECTOR'S TECHNIQUE

One writer has said, "To many in the congregation the director of the choir is a disembodied spirit who materializes for a brief period on Sunday morning and then disappears completely from sight!" They see certain motions of his hands and arms and hear the choir as it responds to these gestures. They can only imagine the mobile expressions of face and eyes which play a major part in good conducting.

To some poeple the arm-waving may at first be disturbing until they come to realize that this is equally as much a part of the choir's anthems as the gestures, body movements, and facial expressions of the pastor's sermon delivery. This action is taken to coordinate the attacks, releases, expression, emphasis, and shadings in tone and volume of singers into one smooth, articulate unit of vocal sound.

The occasional unenlightened minister who may at first object to the director's movements would feel unreasonably curbed if his board should proscribe all gestures and movements in the pulpit.

The skilled director will minimize the movements required to obtain the desired results with his group. Flamboyant attraction of listener attention to himself constitutes cheap "grandstanding" and is inexcusable under any circumstance. The director who may have to overact or exaggerate to get a point across in the rehearsal room will be constantly alert to modify his public technique so that his listeners may enjoy the full benefit of the group's message.

What do all these wavings mean? Is there any rhyme or reason to them?

Yes, they represent definite and clear messages from the leader to his singers. Each movement has a specific significance in guiding the tonal flow. The trained director utilizes this standard language exactly as you and I employ words which to both of us denote particular objects or actions. For example, the first beat in any measure is expressed with a downward stroke or movement of the hand and arm. A separate and distinct pattern is used for each kind of meter, such as the two-four, three-four, four-four, and the six-eight measure.

The entrance, the hold, the increase in volume, the cutoff— each has its own signal. The director who uses this internationally accepted technique is immediately at home with any choir anywhere—provided its former director has given them the proper set of cues.

Full effort can be spent on the music itself without having to waste time in establishing a completely new system of communications. This communication must be as automatic and as instantaneous for director and singer as reactions in driving a car. Only when the technique is learned so thoroughly it can be forgotten can the conductor and his choir establish a true rapport.

Occasionally a young conductor will say, "But I want to be different!" Individualism is most commendable, and is to be encouraged at all times. Young writers feel the same urge, too, but they must still use the language others understand if they are to have readers. The choral director has only to observe the world's great leaders of today to realize their individualism is richly expressed—but within the conventional bounds of common understanding.

Inventing one's own circular gyrations for an increase in volume, or simulating measuring out a yard of ribbon for a hold may be original, interesting, and ego-satisfying to the director, but they are at best disconcerting to the choir and distracting to the congregation or audience. The instrumentalist is completely confused under an unorthodox conductor for the former frequently has to count measures of rest, and he has no full score with the other parts before him. His is a part different from all others, and when he cannot recognize at least the first beat of the measure he is lost.

As a supervisor in a school system so aptly remarked recently, "Some of our young conductors have yet to learn the difference between individualism and peculiarity!"

An appearance of Dr. Lloyd Pfautsch as guest conductor at a combined concert of high school students illustrates the point. Dr. Pfautsch is a veteran of many years of conducting and training both adult and young people's choirs in schools and churches.

In a few short rehearsals he welded 800 students from nine high schools, plus a high school orchestra, into a unit which thrilled both listeners and participants. True, the local directors had done a splendid job of preparing their young singers via memorizing much of the music, but achieving tonal homogeneity, flexibility, and real concerted musicianship from a chorus of this size is a task of considerably greater magnitude.

Technique? His beat was as clear and conventional as any textbook diagram. Completely devoid of superfluous fireworks and temperamental mannerisms, Dr. Pfautsch's leadership was yet alive, dynamic, and inspiring. The standing, cheering ovation accorded him by the young people he had drilled so thoroughly for two and a half days was eloquent evidence of their evaluation of him and his work.

The royal shortcut to success exists no more for conducting than for piano, voice, or any other special field of music. A person may well have spent many years in music study, and still fail as a choral conductor unless he is willing to study, learn, and practice the technique of getting music from others. Of this technique, the arm and hand movements make up but a small portion.

Fortunate is the church whose music leaders possess a balanced background of general and religious music, plus the skill to get others to reproduce this music.

Members of the music committee will frequently find themselves in the situation of being able to enlighten members of the congregation who have not understood what the director is doing. All singers learn rapidly and enjoy more fully the coordinated ensemble effectiveness obtained under skilled leadership.

CHAPTER 6

QUALIFICATIONS OF YOUR ORGANIST

The personal qualifications and basic professional aptitudes of your organist parallel those of your director in many areas. Mere technical proficiency on the instrument forms but a small part of the total requirements for a church organist.

That the organ exists as a part of worship is a premise so obvious as to appear to be beyond question. Its sometime use—or misuse—compels comment here. The organist must always remember that the prelude, offertory, postlude, all sections where he performs alone are integral parts of a worship service, designated to establish, enhance, develop or climax the progress of the hour.

His accompaniment of hymns must be substantial enough to support their singing, yet not overpowering or stifling to their concerted volume. His playing is the framework for the picture, in the choir's anthem.

Should he not, then, have the opportunity to express himself personally on this great instrument as a soloist? Decidedly, yes! At least two, preferably more times a year he should be encouraged, nay, expected to present to the public concerts on this noble instrument. Probably for no other solo instrument is there such rich literature of all grades of difficulty and levels of audience understanding.

Properly encouraged, your organist will provide for you evenings of music which will enrich and inspire your entire community.

Now, of course, when he/she has invested the time and effort to prepare and perfect the concert it is up to the music committee to see that he has a good audience present to hear him, isn't it? I mean, to actually get among the congregation, personally, to make sure his efforts are appreciated. Don't expect him to play these programs for the congregation if they are not out to hear him.

During the services, his work at the keyboard is necessarily subordinated to the ideas of the complete worship unit, and under the control of the director. The latter is, in turn, responsible to the minister for the overall production of the music. After clearly establishing the types and categories of music desired by the church for the service, the wise director will allow the organist to choose the specific numbers to be used, except when church mandate or special occasion may require designated compositions. The organist knows what he/she can play well, and within the above limitations, should be allowed to use his/her initiative in selecting appropriate numbers.

If in rare cases an organist cannot make his/her part of the teamwork fit the requirements of the director, he/she (like the director who cannot cooperate wholeheartedly with the policies of pastor and church) has no place in the church family.

Pride, the kind that spurs the individual to do his best in service to God, we need in every church in the land! Selfless cooperation on the part of the organist, director, yes, and the minister himself is a necessary ingredient in every successful house of worship.

The following rather searching set of questions is the result of a study project on this subject conducted by one of the recent church music administration classes at the University of Texas at El Paso. Made up about equally of directors and organists, the group readily agreed that few candidates would fulfill all requirements. They did also agree, however, that this outline could provide a guide for both the selection of the candidates and the encouragement of further study by incumbents. It was pointed out that many of these questions would be applicable with equal relevance to the director. This, and chapter four may serve as a guide for your selection of new church music leadership. Where several candidates are under consideration the incorporation of these points into a check list for each will facilitate fair comparisons.

Requirements for the Organist

PERSONAL

1. Does he/she have a Christian background, both in educacation and training?
2. Is he/she humble?
3. Is he/she a dedicated Christian?
4. Does he/she possess intestinal fortitude?
5. Is he/she dependable?
6. Is he/she sincere?
7. Does he/she radiate poise and self-confidence?
8. Is he/she emotionally mature?
9. Does he/she have a sense of humor?
10. Are his/her word usage and diction proper?
11. Is he/she tactful and understanding?
12. Does he/she maintain a cooperative attitude toward the director, music committee, board, and pastor?
13. Can he/she take suggestions well?
14. Is he/she punctual?
15. Does he/she inspire others?
16. Is he/she self-disciplined?
17. Are the spouse's occupation and attitude toward the Church appropriate?

PROFESSIONAL

1. Does he/she have a degree?
2. Is he/she educated in church administration and theology?
3. Is his/her academic training sufficient in:

theory	composition
harmony	counterpoint
sight singing	musicology
vocal arranging	arranging

4. Can he/she be prepared to cover for a mistake in the service?
5. Has he/she ever attended any classes in church music?
6. Is he/she capable of selecting worthwhile music?
7. Is he/she willing to play for the music committee?
8. Is he/she willing to play for the choirs and services on a trial basis?
9. Is he/she physically strong?
10. Does he/she believe in clothing the text with music of beauty and vitality?
11. Is he/she able to attend all the needed church functions? This includes weddings and funerals.
12. Is he/she available for rehearsals?
13. Is he/she a stable person within his community? This includes other churches.
14. Does he/she possess a philosophy of church music?
15. Does he/she desire to contribute to the spiritual life of the church?
16. Is he/she willing to continue his/her study for his/her betterment?
17. Does he/she direct his/her attention to the music rather than to himself/herself?
18. Is he/she willing to share his/her knowledge and show initiative?
19. Is he/she opposed to presenting recitals?
20. Does he/she love music?
21. Is he/she proficient in his/her instrument—either electronic or pipe organ?
22. Does he/she have a good background in piano?
23. Does he/she have experience in accompanying?
24. Does he/she give life, emotion, and shape to the hymn tune?
25. Does he/she have knowledge of the human voice?

Qualifications of Your Organist

26. Can he/she modulate smoothly and quickly?
27. Is he/she patient?
28. Is he/she adaptable to change?
29. Does he/she execute the changing of stops quietly and without disturbing the worship of the congregation?
30. Does he/she possess a knowledge of hymn literature and the ability to play each one appropriately?
31. Does he/she work well with others to attain a desired end?
32. Does he/she have training in voice?
33. Does he/she understand the purpose of congregational singing?
34. Does he/she understand the principles of acoustics?
35. Can he/she play by ear?
36. Has he/she worked with many grade levels?
37. Is he/she proficient in accompanying?
38. Is he/she willing to teach organ or piano?
39. Will he/she want to train others in the church?
40. Can he/she direct?
41. Does he/she have a good repertory of appropriate music?
42. What is his/her attitude toward the salary required?
43. Is he/she neat in appearance?
44. Does he/she *enjoy* playing the organ, and to what extent?
45. Why does he/she want this job?
46. What is his/her professional background? (Definite names of places and duties performed.)
47. Can he/she provide a substitute when he/she is absent?

Where complete knowledge of character or attributes may not be obtainable from former employers, full discussion of expectations of your committee with the applicant is in order. With a complete set of mutually accepted requirements and a written contract covering mutual obligations provided for both employer and employee, most of the potential unpleasantness in this relationship can be avoided.

Such questions as number 20 may seem to be belaboring the obvious. To the study group, though, examples of players who have become disenchanted with music itself and who are continuing willy-nilly in their field simply because they cannot make a living in anything else do exist often enough to have this question included.

Questions 14, 16, 21, 23, 25, 30, and 33, for example, are prompted where a brilliant organist may be playing altogether too loudly for congregational singing. Unfortunately this is not as rare as it should be!

Even as the successful business conducts regular inventories, the effective pastor and committee will take time to sit down with the music staff and take stock.

CHAPTER 7

ORGANIST-DIRECTOR?

It should be apparent after reading chapters four and six that both the director and the organist who fill their posts adequately have full-time jobs! However, there still remain a few churches that seek out and employ one person to try to do the work of both. In many cases this is a holdover from the earlier days of our American churches when an organist and a professional quartet were employed to "worship in music" *for* the congregation while the latter sat or stood mutely content.

In other cases the church mistakenly believes that it can "economize" with such a combination. The organist brings forth snatches and sketches of the score before him/her with one hand while he/she attempts to cue in or cut out the voice parts for his/her choir with the other. With both hands on the manuals his/her head nods and sways in an attempt to keep the singers together.

All too frequently a taped record of the service, and sometimes even casual listening discloses that the organ, which should be *accompanying,* is in truth *leading* the singers.

In the accompaniments provided, the composer presupposes the use of both hands and the full attention of the accompanist.

Any experienced conductor will agree that the extraction from the printed page of the fullest capabilities of four or more singing parts with all the phrasing, dynamics, punctuation, and ultimate total musical message requires *all* the techinique of which he/she is capable.

What if the director has a pianist-accompanist for the rehearsal, and then himself/herself "plays" both the organ and choir in public service? Just when his/her singers need him/her most, at least a part of him/her must be given to the organ. You may ask, "If they have learned their parts well on Thursday night shouldn't they be able to perform without obvious leadership on Sunday?" "Yes," I must answer, "but they cannot have the same full measure of confidence and complete attention to the message of the anthem that they do have when their director is actually leading. They will get through it technically rather well sometimes, with a small group, and when that group is totally comprised of professional singers."

Upon the death of Arturo Toscanini, the New York Philharmonic members, all skilled musicians of the highest caliber, who practiced eight hours daily through each week, decided to try to carry on his great tradition without a conductor. After a few less than successful months the experiment was abandoned as a failure. What, then, should we expect of our choristers, most of them amateurs, who get a maximum of *two* hours of practice per *week,* and that at least two days away from their presentation?

The next time someone attempts to persuade you that an organist-director can do the job just as well as two people, ask him to show you how many great choirs and first-rate choruses today use this combination. If this arrangement were more, or even equally effective would not the practice be general? I have talked with a number of good singers who have served under both systems. "Yes, we 'get through' the services, all right," is the usual gist, "but there is not the same cleancut, confident rendition that we have under direction."

Why is it that for special occasions like a television program, a select group appearance, or an oratorio performance with instrumentalists the erstwhile organist-director employs an accompanist so he can direct the ensemble?

To the majority of leaders and governing committees responsible for music in our churches, every service is "special" enough for us to put forth the best quality of worship of which we are capable.

"We have eliminated all the jangling between director and organist. We have hired one person to do it all!" "We find it is much cheaper to hire an organist-director. We don't have a big budget, you know!" These, and other similar rationalizations are quite familiar to the writer. One person *can* do the job after a fashion, it is true. You who choose this arrangement must be prepared to accept its limitations.

We who have observed both situations over many years under many kinds of conditions fail to shake off the conviction that the combination is much like the young man who is driving down the highway with one arm and trying to make love to his sweetheart with the other. He finds it extremely difficult to do a completely satisfactory job in either department!

CHAPTER 8

THE VOLUNTEER CHOIR

"What can you expect from a volunteer choir?" asks the exasperated director after an unhappy experience with some singers who had not learned what real choir responsibility is. Well, what *can* we, or what *should* we expect?

Unfortunately I am forced to the conclusion that haphazard attendance and lack of interest must be blamed equally on the director and the choir in many instances. In such situations the following questions arise: How long has this director been with this group? What steps, over how long a period, has he taken to indoctrinate and educate the choir as to its obligations and privileges? Yes, I said, *"privileges!"* Is not the music leadership of an entire parish a precious privilege?

How does the director treat his individuals? What kind of rehearsal does he run? What is the choir's concept of its job? And, most basic of all, what is the director's *own* philosophy of music in worship?

The following may be difficult to believe, but it is true. In one choir which the writer was employed to take over, the attitude of at least some of the singers had been thus expressed: one morning when the minister came to the choir room for the prayer before the service this remark was overheard, "Does he think we are so wicked he has to come pray over us before he lets us in the church?"

Prayer immediately became a part of the choir's activities. Within three months the officers of the choir were offering these prayers, and within six months *any* member of the group would respond at the request of the vice president (devotions chairman).

Perhaps the first question in this chapter can best be answered by turning to an outline of standards and beliefs adopted by the two older choirs at another church where the writer served. After some weeks of discussion and re-hashing the Chancel Choir (adult) adopted a code. Thereupon the Epworth (high school age) Choir began its own study, using the adult outline as a basis. Below is a reprint of the booklet which the young people published and *used regularly!* In all fairness, it must be told that these young people *stiffened* some of the requisites of their elders! Bracketed words are from the adult outline.

THE MINISTRY OF MUSIC

The Epworth Choir

When you are accepted into the fellowship of the Epworth Choir [Chancel Choir] of _____ Church, you become a member of a group which plays a vital part in the entire worship of the church. This choir sets the atmosphere for the worship service, guides and cooperates with the congregation in its musical participation (hymns and responses), and joins with your minister in making possible a significant and moving worship service for many people each week.

You will have the rich privilege of sharing with the choir a wide range of music from the hearts of both ancient and modern composers. Since the choir ministers to the entire congregation just as the pastor does, our hymns and anthems are widely varied to reach as many worshiping individuals as we can.

You will associate with some of the finest folks you have ever met. If you are warm and friendly you will find their attitude mirroring your own. They are dedicated, serious, and reverent, as you may already have discovered. They also know how to relax and have fun! If you can sing, if you are sincere in your desire to use your talents in God's praise, and you are willing to meet the attendance and effort requirements of the group, then you are most welcome.

Your choir will expect you to be in your assigned seat during regular rehearsal periods and for the Sunday worship hours for which this group is responsible. While extra rehearsal time and other participation is kept to a minimum, you will be expected to make every effort to share these responsibilities when they occur.

When you become one of us, the choir is increased just so much by your capabilities, your cooperation, ideas, and your complete individual personality. If we did not believe that you would make a real contribution to our total combined product of worship to God, we should not permit you to become one of us. If your name is placed on our roll and you become negligent and careless in your obligations, it will be our unpleasant duty to drop you from our membership.

On the other hand, if the time comes when, because of moving away, or some other major change in your living, you must terminate your membership with us, come and tell us directly. We will regretfully but sincerely send you on your way with our blessing.

Any rehearsal important enough to be scheduled is of sufficient importance to require your presence. The public worship each week requires a carefully prepared, thoroughly known and reverently offered presentation. We have found that our weekly rehearsal of one hour [two hours for the adult choir] is the bare minimum required for anything like a satisfactorily prepared unit.

As you sing with us you, too, will realize how difficult it becomes to have to retrace steps already covered because someone else was needlessly absent.

We know that unexpected illness can strike at any time. When you are ill enough to have to miss work or school, then of course we do not expect you to be at choir. By the same token, the reverse is equally true!

Occasionally one's work or school obligations may cause an

The Volunteer Choir

absence. This we accept, too. During the two weeks summer vacation time for the family we understand that you probably will be away from us.

Realistically speaking, we should say that the person who is present for all but five weeks during the year, including vacation, is doing satisfactorily, attendance-wise. Many of our members do better than this, however!

When an overwhelming reason causes you to be absent, we expect you to call your section leader *beforehand* and tell him why you cannot attend. When the section leader cannot be reached a call to the church office will be forwarded to your director. Adjustments must be made whenever your absence changes the balance of the choir. The overall balance which your choir has worked out after you were accepted is thrown off when you are not there. Your associates and your director properly frown upon any absence which would hinder the work of the choir. Most important of all, you are cheating God of a service which you, by joining the choir, have promised to render.

Birthdays and anniversaries are occasions which are worthy of celebration, of course. Since our choir has to lead musically at each Sunday service, absence from regular rehearsal or worship for parties or like activities is to be guided by at least the same consideration which we use for school [work] attendance.

For the same reason, we as choir members agree that our regular rehearsals must take precedence over other meetings or events which may be scheduled at the same time.

For such occasions as church-wide picnics, "Mystery Trips," and Sub-District affairs when each of us takes part, the regular rehearsal will be canceled or postponed.

You who are learning to read music will need practice to bring yourself as rapidly as possible to the quick perception required in assimilating the constant flow of new music which we must prepare. You who are skilled and experienced choristers have a golden opportunity (and the obligation) to pass on the guidance and leadership which was extended to you when you were just learning.

What about accepting the other church obligations while you

are in the choir? This is most praiseworthy *when it can be accomplished without interference with choir duties or the strength and hours required for choir engagements!* We are proud of the fact that many of our members are among the leaders of our church life.

The thinking leaders of your church, beginning with your pastor, realize the vital importance of the choir in our regular worship. Accordingly, they avoid meetings or other activities on scheduled rehearsal nights or periods which might in any way conflict with the proper functioning of these groups. Of no other group in your church is required the *constant* proficiency in public presentation, at the exact specified hour and minute, and with the same sustained degree of finish and reverence that our worshipers rightfully expect of us.

When there is any question in your mind about the significance of the choir, just look into the congregation and see for yourself the number of reasons why you and your best are needed regularly.

Each new candidate for the choir must complete a probationary period of three consecutive weeks before being accepted into full membership.

To the inexperienced person our requirements may at first appear to be somewhat rigorous. We do not believe, however, in bringing to our God the leavings after everything else which may at the moment be more appealing than choir. We believe that He created us; that He made possible all the blessings of life which we enjoy; and that we are returning to Him just a small measure of the praise and honor which are rightfully His!

We shall be proud and happy to have you as one of us. We know that you will share the blessings, the enjoyment and the rich sense of wellbeing which comes from giving of one's self to serve others.

Our all-covering creed is short and simple:
To our Lord—only our best!
(End of booklet)

The Volunteer Choir

Another approach to this question of dedication and participation is as follows. This application agreement, covenant, and constitution are in successful operation in other churches.

APPLICATION FOR CHOIR MEMBERSHIP

Miss
Name (print) Mr. _____ Birthday_____
　　　　　Mrs.　(Last)　　　(First)
Home Address_____ Phone_____
Business Address_____ Phone_____
Are you a Christian?_____ Member of what church?_____
Member this Sunday school___Play instrument?___What?_____
Voice part_____Sing solos?_____Sing in ensembles?_____
Date of Application_____ Accepted_____
If not, why? _____

CHOIR MEMBER'S COVENANT
(Please read carefully)

As a member of the Sanctuary Choir of _____ Church, located in _____, I recognize the opportunity to serve Christ by singing His message and His praise. My effectiveness in this area of His service is dependent upon faithfulness in this choral organization. I want this choir to present the finest choral music possible, and realize that such can be produced only by rehearsed singers. I will be present for every rehearsal and service at which the choir sings, unless ill or providentially hindered; and will not expect to sing in a performance after missing the preceding rehearsal without consulting the director. More than one unreported absence per month will justify removal of my name from the choir membership and the assignment of my music and robe to another.

Date_____　　_____
　　　　　　　　　　　　　　　　　　(Signature)

CHECK LIST FOR NEW MEMBERS

_____ Auditioned by Director
_____ Membership vice president for introduction to choir

_____ Choir name tag made
_____ Introduced to section group captain and entered on group list
_____ Name added to section attendance chart
_____ Membership card made up and put in roll book
_____ Music assigned by librarian
_____ Robe assigned by robe chairman

Music number_____Assigned by_____(Librarian)
Robe number_____Assigned by_____(Robe chairman)
      Height_____ Robe size_____

AGREEMENT AND CONSTITUTION
of the
Sanctuary Choir, _____ _____ Church

AGREEMENT

1. That music is an essential to worship, not a decoration or luxury.
2. That the works of great composers are none too good to use in the worship of God. The best selections that possibly can be found should be used in preference to a lesser caliber of music.
3. Those who are to interpret this music should do so honestly and sincerely. We, therefore, covenant together to keep our spiritual lives strong and effective that we may be able to be used of God through our music.
4. To do this we earnestly agree to practice prayer and forgiveness, and to keep our hearts free from ill will toward all people, particularly toward other choir members.

CONSTITUTION

Article One: Name

The name of this organization shall be the Sanctuary Choir of the_____ _____Church of_____ _____

Article Two: Membership

A. Any person desiring membership in the choir will make ap-

The Volunteer Choir

plication to the membership vice president, with final approval of the director.
B. Full membership is attained only after the following steps have been taken:
   1. Application is completed and the covenant read and signed.
   2. Personal interview with the classification committee.
   3. Introduction to section leader and name placed on his records.
   4. Constitution thoroughly read and understood.
   5. Music and robe assignments made.
C. Every member of the choir must be seventeen years of age or older.

Article Three: Officers and Leaders

A. The choir shall elect officers annually in October.
B. Appointive positions such as committee chairmen, section leaders, etc., shall also be filled annually, appointed by the president on recommendation by the executive committee.
C. The executive committee shall be composed of the elected officers of the choir.
D. The elected officers shall be: president, membership vice president, fellowship vice president, secretary-treasurer, robe chairman, librarian.
E. Suggested qualifications for elected officers: enthusiastic, diplomatic, energetic, possessing executive ability and a vital interest in church music.

Article Four: Duties of Officers

A. President—He shall serve as the executive officer of the choir and serve as chairman of the executive committee. He shall appoint the necessary committees and will work with the pastor and minister of music to make an outstanding organization which will be a distinguished asset to the entire church program. He is an ex-officio member of all committees and has general oversight of the choir's business.
B. Membership Vice-president—He succeeds the president in his absence and must have access to a telephone. As chairman

of the membership committee, composed of elected or appointed section leaders, it is his duty to see that the committee functions in keeping the membership reports concerning attendance of individuals, sections, and the entire choir; totals and percentages.
C. Fellowship Vice-president—His primary responsibility is that of fostering friendship and good fellowship among the membership. He is responsible for the orientation of all new members. He introduces new members to the choir and cares for the needs of visitors at rehearsal. He is responsible for the choir's social activities. He will make arrangements for nursery facilities for special occasions.
D. Secretary-treasurer—He is the recorder of business and comptroller of choir funds. He is responsible for adequate publicity and advertising of special performances. At the direction of the president the secretary-treasurer purchases and dispatches appropriate remembrances to ill or bereaved choir members. He publicizes and receives the monthly offering which is the source of revenue for these remembrances and for social functions.
E. Robe chairman—As chairman of the robe committee, he is directly responsible for issuance, repair and appearance of robes.
F. Librarian—A chairman of the library committee, he/she is directly desponsible for issuance of all music used by the choir. He/she must see that all music is in good repair, adequately filed and indexed, distributed and collected at rehearsals and performances.

Article Five: Committees, Their Members and Function
A. Executive Committee: President is chairman. Other elected officers also are members. The executive committee meets monthly or at the discretion of the president and plans the program of the choir. It coordinates the work of the choir with the entire program of the church.
B. Membership Committee: Membership vice-president is chairman. Section leaders complete the committee. The section leaders are responsible for a complete and accurate record

of the attendance of the choir membership assigned to them. It is from these records that the membership vice-president makes his monthly report to the choir. The section leaders must maintain a complete list of membership assigned to them, with full names, addresses, phone numbers, places of business, and business phones. Each section leader is responsible for the regular attendance of his section and should inspire his members to the best possible record. He will notify the president in the event of sickness or death in the immediate family of a choir member. He will sometimes be required to visit within the choir membership.

C. Social Committee: Fellowship vice-president is chairman. Other members are selected by the chairman. The committee fosters good fellowship among the membership and is responsible for all the social events of the choir.

D. Robe Committee: Robe chairman is chairman. One member from each voice section is appointed by the president to comprise this committee when necessary. Each maintains a list of the membership of his section with their height, robe size, and robe number assigned. The committee is responsible for the maintenance, cleanliness, and general appearance of the robes of the choir.

E. Library Committee: Librarian is chairman. Three members appointed by the president comprise this committee. It is responsible for the issuance of all music and hymnals used by the choir, and for adequate cataloguing, filing, indexing, distribution, and collection of all music used at rehearsals and performances.

F. Nominating Committee: appointed by the president.

(End of Covenant)

It will be noted in the foregoing type of organization that choir members themselves assume more of the housekeeping duties. Many choir members do not feel that they can give the additional time beyond that of the rehearsals and services.

The music committee has a weighty obligation to the church and its music groups in educating its members gradually but steadily into the proper concept of true choir stewardship.

Volunteering for the army or navy does not mean that one may choose the battles in which he will fight, and those from which he prefers to abstain. So in the choir, membership must be understood to mean participation in *all* the service of the organization for a definite period, preferably units of not less than a year.

The Volunteer Choir

The job is not easy in these days of parental overpermissiveness and prevalent laissez faire attitude. We must teach our young people *and* adults, though, that once our promise is made, the obligation is as binding for appearance without remuneration as it would be were we to receive $100 for each service!

Will the music committee and director ever make this program work one hundred percent? Definitely not. However, just as surely as the pastor knows he will never eradicate sin in its entirety, but still keeps on working to bring it down as far as possible, so positively must the committee and director aim steadily toward the goal of one hundred percent dedication for members of all choirs.

The director will need all the support he can get from every member of the committee in the relentless campaign of bringing home the importance and the seriousness of dedication and faithful participation on the part of *all* choir members.

What director has not been approached by the type of person who self-righteously offers, "I'll be glad to help you out at Christmas and Easter time, but I'm too busy to sing regularly with the choir!" The writer's reply to these individuals? "If you are 'too busy' to use your voice in God's praise the rest of the year, I'm sure you will be all the more so at the holiday times! The choir's part in worship is just as vital in February and June as it is on December 25th, so we'll manage to get along with our regular members."

Our year-round, faithful choirs are far better off without the Johnny- or Susie-come-lately type who like to be "in on" the times when there might be a bit more glory or prominence, but who fail utterly to comprehend what the choir means to the worship service. These folks are first cousins to those who dress up and go to church on Easter and Christmas Sundays and evidently think thereby to soak up enough grace to last the rest of the year!

Your regular choir members appreciate such loyalty of their director as much as they do his emphatic *no* to persons who would gladly come and sing a solo once in a while, but couldn't possibly sing with the choir regularly!

It is fervently hoped that the committee and the pastor will maintain a solid front of support for the director's policy in decisions of this sort, no matter how glamorous or influential the shallow "would be's" may be.

This policy certainly does *not* apply to the former members home from school for the holidays and who head for the choir the first thing on arrival in town! Their joy at being back is shared by everyone, and somehow there can be arranged the extra coaching and instruction required to ready them for the services involved.

The citing of just a few of the problems which beset a director may serve to show our committeemen how much they need to support him as he strives to follow the credo "To Our Lord—Only Our Best!"

CHAPTER 9

THE ADULT CHOIR

What Is a Chorister?

When a person joins his chancel choir he demonstrates to his fellow men that he possesses many outstanding characteristics. He likes people. In turn his associates enjoy his company. He has strength of character. It takes precise self-control to combine one's vocal output with that of others at the split second, same volume, and like shade of tone color.

This same forcefulness brings him regularly to Thursday night rehearsal and Sunday worship lest he miss his share of the joy of great sacred music. He can, and does say, "No," to glittering diversions. He is colorful. When he sings, he verily *is* for the moment prophet, disciple, supplicant, or narrator, as vocal praise to God pours from his being. He is a keen judge of values. From his erstwhile seat in the pew, even as you, he has realized how much more he could give to, and get from his worship in this choir. He is generous. He will extend to you the warm hand of fellowship as you make the decision to join strength to strength in this great experience!

"What Is a Chorister?" and other similar brief messages were folded in the morning bulletins for the congregation at intervals of several months. Following each such broadcast we gained either new members or people who wanted to receive training to read music and sing.

The heart of any church's music program is its adult choir. Leading the congregation in the music of worship, this group can set and maintain the atmosphere of the entire worship period.

In one church where the author served the adult choir was at first opposed to any kind of organization or election of officers. As one singer later said, "I thought we were headed for being just another social group, and I was against it!"

One evening the entire organization of the music committee was explained, including the desirability of having a representative of the adult choir in its membership. All the items that needed "someone's" time and energy were discussed. Before we adjourned we had our four conventional officers: president, vice-president, secretary, treasurer. It was pointed out to the choir how little time for music itself the director would have if he alone were to undertake the discharge of details given below. This following proved to be one workable distribution of duties.

Duties of the Adult Choir Personnel

A. President
  1. Coordinates the entire choir program (under guidance of the music director).
  2. Music committee liaison. The choir president automatically becomes a member of the church music committee and remains as such until his successor has been duly elected.
B. Vice-president
  1. Membership. Membership chairman (below) is directly responsible to him.
  2. Choir devotions. Arranges for different members of choir to offer the prayers at rehearsals and before worship services.
  3. Public relations. Responsible for keeping papers, church paper, other media informed as to newsworthy activities of the choir.

The Adult Choir

   4. Special projects. Organizes required details for such projects as choir participation in the church fair, making of recordings, choir trips, choir study retreats.
   5. Presides at business meetings in absence of the president.
C. Secretary
   1. Correspondence.
      a. All correspondence is cleared through, and recorded by the secretary.
      b. He keeps file copies of all correspondence, including that of director, and others pertaining to adult choir projects and business.
      c. Sends "get well," "thanks," and other similar communications as directed and keeps appropriate record thereof.
      d. Answers letters addressed to the choir, upon action and instruction of the group.
   2. Maintains *current* list of names, addresses, telephones of all members, from membership chairman.
   3. Keeps minutes of all business meetings, record of all projects engaged in by the choir.
D. Treasurer
   1. Keeps record of all choir finances not included in church budget.
      a. Bank deposits and withdrawals
      b. Income and disbursements
         (1) Gifts, flowers, cards
         (2) Special projects of the choir
   2. Makes financial reports for executive council and full choir as required.
E. Membership Chairman
   1. Keeps current file of active and inactive members.
   2. Provides additions, corrections (addresses and telephones), drops, (*as soon as they occur*) to the following:
      a. Director   d. Robe Chairman
      b. Secretary   e. Librarian
      c. Section Leader
      Note: The importance of making a needed robe available to another waiting member, or of getting the li-

brarian to make the new folder immediately seems obvious. Sometimes it will be the director who notifies the membership chairman. Then the latter must inform the others concerned.
3. Keeps roll on Sundays, rehearsals, and special occasions.
   a. Section leaders hand chairman list of absentees of their own sections.
   b. Section leader thus maintains complete record of individual, sectional, and total choir attendance for use of director.
4. Notifies director of advance absences when provided.

F. Robe Chairman
1. Measures each member, adjusts robe to fit. Usually has an assistant who is a seamstress or is capable of running a sewing machine.
2. Assigns robes, collars, and accessories and maintains a current *posted* list of issued and non-assigned robes and equipment.
3. Ascertains that *permanent* number and temporary name tag are present in each issued robe.
4. Supervises cleaning and repair of all robes and accessories.
   Note: In some churches robes are cleaned at stated intervals "in toto." In others individuals have their own robes cleaned as desired. White collars are usually cleaned and ironed by the women to whom issued.
5. Supervises donning, doffing, and proper hanging in closets.
   Note: Some members have to be reminded from time to time as to proper methods of using and caring for their robes—even adults!

G. Librarian. Responsible for all music of the choir
1. Records on folder or card, or both:
   a. Complete information of the selection: title, composer, classification
   b. Number of copies
   c. When received
   d. Price (per unit)
   e. When performed
2. Stamps and numbers each copy.
   Note: An increasing number of choirs prefer to have

The Adult Choir

       the measures of each anthem numbered for quick reference in rehearsal.
   3. Has music ready for services and rehearsals.
   4. Checks folders and music in and out to members for home study.
   5. Files and stores music, maintains cross-reference.
      a. Cross-indexing (one file of cards for each)
         (1) Composition title
         (2) Composer
         (3) Classification
H. Properties Chairman
   1. Has rehearsal room in proper order for each meeting.
      a. Lights
      b. Temperature and ventilation
      c. Chairs, music stands, and other equipment arranged
   2. Sanctuary
      a. Chairs or seats provided for choir and director prior to *each service*
      b. Any special equipment needed for service
      c. Reserving pews (with ushers) for other choirs or personnel before the service
   3. Special occasions
      a. Orchestra lights on stands for choirs or players
      b. Arranging special lighting or audio equipment
      c. Installing, using, and *returning* equipment.
I. Section Leader (soprano, alto, tenor, bass)
   1. Reports to membership chairman on absentees.
   2. Greets, introduces, seats new members.
   3. Sees that music is provided each new member.
   4. Checks appearance of section at worship.
      a. Condition and proper wearing of robe
      b. Absence of earrings or other extraneous jewelry
   5. Assists director with discipline and courtesies of section members when requested or when appropriate.
   6. Calls all absentees as soon as possible after session—no *later* than following day.
J. Telephone Chairman
   1. Keeps members informed (usually through section leaders)

of special events, extra or changed rehearsals, and other pertinent matters.
   2. Calls non-member individuals, organizations, as needed.
K. Nursery and Babysitting Chairman

   1. Arranges for nursery to be open, heated, ready as required.
      a. Designated rooms, cribs, equipment (play)
   2. Assists with recruiting, keeping list of available personnel.
   3. Notifies and reminds personnel as required.
   5. Maintains service and employment record with church office where sitters are paid.
L. Social Chairman
   1. Arranges post-rehearsal refreshment upon occasion as determined.
   2. Manages social events as determined by choir.
   3. Checks "pulse" of choir to ascertain when a social function may be beneficial.
   4. Works with director on social sections of choir retreats, camps, and similar functions.

All officers and chairmen are responsible for their particular functions. Each, himself, must arrange for an alternate to function for him when an absence becomes necessary. He may not just call the director or president and say, "I'm ill and cannot be present. You will have to get someone else to act for me tonight!"

The Adult Choir

Each chairman is encouraged to enlist whatever aid he may wish or need to do his job effectively. The important thing is that his portion of the team project be done fully and well!

* * * * *

The following is a matter of policy, to be decided ultimately by the pastor and director, but a comment may not be out of line. Some churches admit only church members to their adult and youth choirs, while others admit individuals to choir membership regardless of profession or non-profession of faith.

The writer has served churches of both preferences. He has reached the conclusion that, in his estimation, the latter policy is much to be preferred. Time after time, it has happened that individuals who first came to the choir solely because they loved to sing have become imbued with the dedication and spirit of reverence of their fellow choristers. They have discovered at first hand what Christian devotion is. They have made the decision that they wish Christ to be their Savior, too, and have publicly made this declaration for church membership.

CHAPTER 10

AGE-GROUP CHOIRS

It is by no accident that age-group choirs are growing in number and size throughout our country today. Not intended for parading "cute" youngsters before the congregation or "dressing up" the worship service, this great movement has a much deeper and more far-reaching significance.

Leaders in major denominational headquarters are quick to agree that an age-group program carried on consistently over a period of years is the most fruitful means of evangelism that a church can have. How has this activity come to rank so high on the list of attributes of a well-rounded church program?

What is an age-group choir? This term means simply the grouping of boys and girls or young people of similar ages and stages of development together to sing as a unit.

While some of our largest city churches in America boast choirs corresponding to nearly every school grade level, the more common and feasible groupings consist of grades 1, 2, and 3 together in the first, or primary choir, and grades 4, 5, and 6 in the second, or intermediate choir. Wherever possible, the junior high grades 7 and 8, and the senior high singers have separate choirs.

Quite frequently the boys with changing voices are shepherded

Age-Group Choirs

into one organization while their sisters sing in another. Naturally, much depends upon the available qualified directors and on the number of singers in the church. Some churches also have college-age or young career-age choirs in addition to the conventional adult groups.

The first benefits thought of are the obvious ones: the learning of the beautiful music of the church, provision of additional singing groups to participate in the worship services, and training "feeders" for the adult choirs.

Other more fundamental justifications are these: boys and girls early develop habits of attending and participating in the activities of the church. They learn the meaning of, and the reason for genuine worship.

They learn that worship is effective only to the degree the individual himself participates. They learn that the church cannot exist by itself in some vague, "somebody-takes-care-of-it" manner, but that it requires the work, means, and support of many families channeled into a single, concerted effort.

It stimulates and holds the interest of the child in church affairs and produces a loyalty and concern which lasts into his adulthood.

Pastors and directors are realizing more and more that excellent choirs do not just "happen." How often in earlier years the writer has encountered a director who was quite satisfied with his adult group and who did not wish to "bother with" the children's choirs, or go out of his way to develop trained leaders for his younger singers. Suddenly, however, when natural attrition of age, moving away, having babies, and change of interests has whittled the number of adult choristers down to an alarming minimum, he has belatedly grasped at stopgap panaceas.

We who enjoy fruit know that the very young tree must first be grafted with the kind of fruit scion desired, then planted and tended during several years of growth before it is ready to produce for us.

The processes of developing good Christians is surprisingly parallel. The church that provides means whereby the children become a needed and recognized part of its worship and life will find them continuing their support and participation as adults. Habits of church attendance, worship participation, financial and

Age-Group Choirs

personal support are strongly established by the time the young people are ready to make their own homes.

"Oh," you say, "but so many of our young people move away, or marry someone away, and we lose them!" Well, that is true, but what about the *other* young folks, couples, who move *into* your community? A good many of my adult choir members have been products of younger choirs in other cities and villages. "We've been in the choir since we can remember. When we moved, I guess we just have naturally gravitated to the church where music is a meaningful part of worship, and where we can go on doing the things which have meant so much to us spiritually." "Our baby is as much at home in the church nursery as he is in his own bed!" "We want to join a church where there are choirs for our young people. We've always been active in singing and we want our own children to have this privilege."

The lay sponsor of each choir is constantly alert to help the director in reaching promptly the new families in the community.

Many families are first reached by the church through their children. As the boys and girls become identified with, and a part of the active life of the church many parents whose background has not included church-going find themselves becoming willing, then enthusiastic partners in this great experience.

Most important of all, however, is the fact that as they live together, practicing and learning and understanding the principles which Christ taught, more and more boys and girls come to take Him as their personal Savior.

The self-discipline involved in regular attendance, loyalty, putting forth one's best efforts, and subjugating personal interest to the welfare of the group are by-products essential to any walk of life.

If there is any question concerning the desirability of an age-group choir system in a church, it surely boils down to this: "How can a church afford *not* to have such a program?"

Several other texts outline most effectively additional advantages of these choirs, so let us proceed to what the music committee can do about them. The music director surveys the community to determine in which age brackets there is the greatest number of available children. Church school attendance should be a strong clue in this direction. For example, in a "young" area made up largely of more recently-marrieds, the logical group would probably be the primary choir, or first, second, and third graders. When he has determined in which category he is going to set up the first "age group" one committee member is selected to help in organizing the group and maintaining its interest and participation.

This person will represent this choir on the music committee. Others, adults or young people, will be selected to assist him in the various ways later outlined. While actual members of the older choirs can and should hold some of the posts of responsibility, it is obvious that more *adult* assistance will be needed in the lower age brackets.

As we continue into the consideration of the choirs in this program the following outline of key personnel for each choir is suggested. Each committeeman directly responsible for a choir will wish one of these sheets for his own use, and will provide one for the director of music. He makes a revised sheet for both himself and the director as personnel changes occur. The addition of individual telephone numbers provides an instant reference which will save many valuable minutes when someone must be called in a hurry. For some of the choirs not all of the categories will apply. For example, "choir mothers" will not be needed for the adult groups, and the division into the four voice parts will not apply to the youngest choirs where unison and two-part singing are the rule.

It should be obvious that such assignment of duties can best be worked out by director and committeeman *together* over a period of a few weeks. Each will be discovering some particular qualifications or traits which will fit certain persons for certain jobs. You may be sure your director will bless you for all the assistance you can give him here!

MINISTRY OF MUSIC

Organization_____ Date_____
Time of meeting_____ Place_____
                day   hour

Age-Group Choirs

Director_____ Accompanist_____
Officers: Pres._____ Vice Pres._____
         Sec._____ Treas._____
Section Leaders: Sop._____ Alto_____
                 Tenor_____ Bass_____
Activity Leaders (first named is chairman)
  Attendance: _____ _____ _____
  Library: _____ _____ _____
  Robes: _____ _____ _____
  Transport: _____ _____ _____
  Telephone: _____ _____ _____
  Nursery: _____ _____ _____
  Social: (Inc.
    refreshments) _____ _____ _____
  Properties: _____ _____ _____
  Choir Mothers:_____ _____ _____
  Other: _____ _____ _____

The High School Choir

With the guidance of one, or possibly two adults, the young people of this age are themselves quite capable of performing the committee responsibilities outlined for the adult choir. These committees will nearly parallel the senior group, with the exclusion of the nursery. As a matter of fact, the training in committee procedures and responsibilities is an essential part of the growing up of these young people.

Getting the committees formed will be the easiest part of all, for this is the age of "joining" or "belonging." Keeping the young people constantly at their obligations will be quite another thing! With the pressures of so many attractive outside demands facing them so insistently today, firm but understanding guidance is required to prevent ineffectual dabbling and frittering.

Follow-up by telephone or direct conversation to see that individual responsibilities are completed is a must! The adult music member has to be understanding of young people and the emotional conflicts of adolescence and still be firm enough to see that committees and individuals function properly and carry through.

This adult is often a parent of one of the choir members who has a personal interest in the welfare of the choir. His (or her) presence at the rehearsal is an invaluable assistance to the director. He relieves the latter of the job of taking roll and checking

on absentees. An immediate telephone call to the home has been found to be most effective in minimizing such absences. Where there is bona fide illness, such a call demonstrates the genuine interest of the group in the individual. Where only a lame excuse or none at all exists, the message soon gets through that the choir means business. The effectiveness of such measures lies in both the promptness and the sureness of such checking. Slipping into the church office and calling the home immediately after roll is taken is by far the best way to cut down on absences.

Age-Group Choirs

This attendance taking and record keeping is a time-robber of precious rehearsal minutes when the director has to do it. It is essential, though, and can be one of the deciding factors in the success of the choir.

It should be remembered that the developing of a genuine sense of responsibility and follow-through of declared intention is a factor far more important than just having a fine-sounding choir! These young people want and need the discipline of a seriously run unit, and when it is administered with love and understanding the experience will never be forgotten.

Remaining through the entire church season is a principle to be insisted upon. Then if the member just has to do something else he can feel that he has fulfilled one obligation before assuming another.

Personnel wall charts by sections, maintained by section leaders, are a matter of pride. Many high schoolers will pooh-pooh the idea, but you just put up a card with a mispelled name and see how soon you get a reaction! When these 3x5 cards have the member's picture up in the corner the importance of the board is enhanced. With a polaroid camera, snapshots of four or five singers can be taken and individual "heads" cut out for the cards.

A little thing? Perhaps. Try it for a year, then accidentally—on purpose—forget to put the cards up next fall. You'll hear from it! These cards also help everyone in the group (including the director) learn names more quickly.

The strengthening of Christian principles at this age goes a long way toward the withstanding of the doubts and assailing forces of the period of the late teens and early twenties. These young people have an organization which *needs* them, which gives them a solid sense of "belonging," and provides an ideal outlet for the "gang" proclivities of the age.

The main function within the choir where other adult help may be required will probably be the robe committee. At least one person skilled in sewing, hemming, and clothing repair will be needed in this important office. This robe-mother frequently becomes a much-loved as well as a critically needed member of the team.

The committee member has a current, firsthand knowledge of the affairs, needs, and progress of the group, and can bring to the general committee meeting a reliable picture of this choir's part in the whole program.

This choir representative should not be unprepared to discover that his greatest problem will be with the parents and not their children! Especially in matters of supporting regular attendance and transportation will he find some of them to be making the lamest of excuses, and to be the most lethargic. In some cases the writer has been forced to the conclusion that our youngsters do a pretty good job of acquitting themselves *in spite* of their parents, rather than because of them!

How can parents insist on regular attendance at school, proper sleeping hours, periodic visits to the dentist, adequate dietary content, and then blindly ignore the most vital part of the youngster's life, his *spiritual* growth? "Oh, we are letting Jim decide on whether or not he goes to church." By what disastrous distortion of logic are these children deemed to be more capable of deciding what or how much spiritual training they should have than whether they should attend school?

Why should these same parents be dismayed or heartbroken when later their youth fail to meet moral dilemmas successfully?

Music committeemen can help to widen the influence of the music program in encouraging parents to begin to give at least as much attention to the spiritual development of their boys and girls as they do to their physical and mental growth.

The more each layman understands the profound importance and the far-reaching results of participation in the younger choirs, the more diligently he will work to promote this vital program.

Social Activities of the High School Choir

No complete accord exists on the amount and kind of social functions, extra parties, or get-togethers a high school choir should have. Students of this age are learning to live with each other, to give and take as young men and women. As with any other choir, this organization basically is *not* a social one. It would appear to be logical, however, that inter-acquaintance, pride in the choir, and just having fun under proper guidance comprise sufficient reasons for getting together in the best possible channeling of the "gang" feeling which is so characteristic of this age.

Held during seasons of the church year when choir interest may be lower than at others, these social meetings may well be extremely desirable. During the summer, combination retreats

78   *The Church Music Handbook*

or weekends for study and good times have already proven their worth.

The music committee and its director and pastor can together work out plans for social affairs which will be a definite asset to the choir's growth and regular attendance.

The Junior High School Choir

As with the senior high school choir, many of the committee functions can be fulfilled by the choir members themselves. The adult sponsor (committee member) will have to provide more detailed guidance in committee organization and procedures, but youngsters of this age are just "trying their wings" and can accomplish surprising things—surprising to uninitiated adults, that is!

Actually *doing* things with their hands is still paramount with this age of young persons. For example, the transportation committee will enjoy mounting a city map on a large corrugated cardboard backing and letting each member install his own flag in its proper location. Each flag consists of a pin with a strip of light cardboard with member's name on one side and the street address on the other. Car pools are thus more easily organized, and less trouble is experienced in providing for the "new" member.

The sponsor (or his adult assistant) should set up and keep a record of the parental "turns" to be sure that the load of driving is equally divided. Most parents are conscientious, but some will conveniently "forget" that it is their turn to serve. One popular arrangement is for Parent A to be responsible for his load for February rehearsals, Parent B to take the load for the February church appearances. Then two others in the group of five or six take the following month, and so on. Sometimes one set of parents will prefer to provide the "taxi" for all the choir's rehearsals and appearances for the month.

An adult assistant for this committee will have considerably more success in arranging schedules than the younger choir member. It is not nearly so easy for a lazy parent to say "no" to another parent!

While setting up the room for rehearsal, arranging needed folders and hymn books, and telephoning can be done by the members, an adult librarian will be required to record, number, and help keep track of music copies.

As with the high school choir one adult with sewing experience will be needed to care for the robe hem lines that were just right in June, but are "every which way" after a summer's growth! Then, too, even the best of choir members have to be reminded occasionally how to hang up their robes!

Fourth, Fifth, Sixth Grade Choir

As the age levels go lower, the amount of additional adult help required by the sponsor automatically increases. On the other hand, there are not as many phases of this program as there are in the adult group.

Young parents are still willing to get their youngsters to and from choir—it has not yet become a "tiresome chore" that it may

JUNE SEPTEMBER

be after a few more years. More adult help is usually more easily obtained for this choir and for the primary one.

One bright thought is that parents who have established the habit of accepting the choir as a part of the family program more easily continue in the "routine" than the newer ones.

The two youngest choirs seldom participate in the worship service more than once a month, which helps to simplify transportation.

Robe chairman, librarian, attendance, transportation, and telephone personnel can help the sponsor immeasurably in these two choirs.

The older youngsters in this age group are approaching puberty and will require all the ingenuity of the music director and his associates to keep them interested in the music program. The voice-changing phenomenon challenges the utmost in us as leaders to "keep them singing" through this age and safely into the high school age.

The bell choir has proved itself as a strong assistant to the director who is striving to keep the interest as the voices start changing.

Primary Choir

In the younger choirs the principal functions needed to be performed by the adult sponsor and his assistants include membership and attendance, robes, librarian (not extensive where so much of the music is learned by rote), telephone, and transportation. Parties for these ages are important but simpler in nature, and are often arranged and supervised by one of the above persons.

Recruiting members for this choir is no problem. Walking into the first grades of the church school (after prior arrangement with the superintendent and teacher, of course!) and asking, "Who would like to sing in the choir?" more often than not brings an instantaneous and unanimous sea of hands. An efficient group of choir mothers under the leadership of the chairman can do much to insure the success of this vital beginning group.

Where a junior church is organized both the primary and the intermediate choirs often present for it the same numbers or anthems which have been prepared and used in the adult hour for that month. This not only adds to the service and gives the singers reason for being but also enhances the choir as an organization in the eyes of the other boys and girls.

The adult assistant should be available to help with handling the hymnals. "But," you admonish, "so many of these primary children cannot yet read!" This is quite true, of course. However, these boys and girls are most insistent on their need of carrying the hymnals into church. They feel more "grown up" this way!

One Sunday morning as our primary choir started down the center aisle I noticed a growing wave of smiles on one side of the aisle. These smiles appeared to be concentrated about one tiny chap as he passed each set of pews. Stepping to the side of the church I could observe why! Singing his heart out on the memorized processional, he was carrying his hymnal proudly in the prescribed manner—but upside down!

CHAPTER 11

CONGREGATIONAL SINGING

The committeeman who assists the music director in this field has one of the most critical lay jobs in the entire church.

How many churchgoers have discovered that, next to their Bible, their denominational hymnal comprises the greatest single source of comfort, courage, and inspiration available to them? Between the hymnal's covers we find the thoughts of the greatest poets of the ages. Set to the stirring melodies and harmonies of equally inspired composers, the combinations which we call hymns are capable of lifting us out of our everyday selves and bringing us into closer touch with our Creator.

The hymn belongs neither to the minister nor the choir. It is the express property of the individual worshiper. It has been written for him. It is his means of self-expression. He who would quail at the thought of having to express his convictions on his feet or who is stricken speechless at the thought of having to voice a prayer before his fellow men will often join fervently with his neighbors in voicing his praise to God through a familiar verse set to a long-known and well-known and loved tune!

Since earliest recorded history, at least, man has used his

voice in worship to his known and unknown gods. Crude and primitive as they were at first, his utterances nevertheless became accepted and integral parts of the homage and sacrifices which he paid his deities.

As worship gradually assumed some regular forms and procedure the combinations of words and expressed thoughts kept pace. The growth of the concept of one God brought about a development of vocal expressions of worship of priests and communicants alike.

There have been periods in history during which exclusive intermediaries carried on the formal liturgies of spiritual relationship with the Divine Being. The common man, however, has had a way of repeatedly swinging the pendulum back where he, himself, could find satisfaction in communicating directly with his God.

In this practice of establishing and re-establishing a direct kinship with Jehovah, the common man and his leaders have composed some of the most effective poem-songs we know today.

The choir today does have its special musical message through its anthem, and it leads in responses and introits. Its most important job remains, however, the leading, the instructing, and assisting the congregation in their hymns. The choir is itself of the congregation, and it must never forget its privilege of ministry to *all* of the congregational worship through these hymns.

"A Mighty Fortress Is Our God" was not called the "battle hymn of the Reformation" for nothing. Its staunch words and Gibraltar-rock-like chorale melody rallied untold thousands to Luther's side as he fearlessly labored to correct existing evils and return corporate and individual worship to the common man.

The Roman Catholic Church has just taken a gigantic step forward in vernacularizing its liturgy and its music. Thus can the single communicant in any country understand and make the worship truly his own. It is to be fervently hoped, however, that the rich heritage of chants gathered, purified, and promulgated by Pope Gregory may still be perpetuated in their traditional beauty and effectiveness. Tragic, indeed, would be any watering-down, "adaptations," or other attempts to "popularize" them!

It would obviously require many pages to trace our present hymnology through the chant, plainsong and subsequent forms which have evolved to the present day. Fascinating volumes are available. (See Appendix.) The discharge of non-musical duties by your lay music personnel will enable your director to bring more of this information to your people.

Our primary interest lies in the use we make of our hymns and sacred songs today. Empty and barren would be our services today without the congregational singing of hymns of adoration, confession, supplication, and dedication. Many more of our lay group today are finding added meaning in sharing the musical responses and introits in their worship.

The erasing of worldly cares for the hour of close communion with God, the lifting of the soul in praise for our many blessings, preparation of the mind and heart for the spoken message, affirmation of resolve to higher achievement—these and many other goals may be approached and attained through the pages of your hymnal.

The music of the service, as typified principally by the congregational hymn, goes hand in hand with the spoken message to make up a complete experience in worship. It is important, therefore, that the hymns be chosen as carefully as the text is selected for the sermon.

Does the preacher take his Bible and read from just any page, here or there, which happens to fall open? This wouldn't make much sense, would it? Is it any more logical just to sing "something" from the hymnal? The results *can* be just as chaotic! One pastor was understandably shocked to discover in the Sunday bulletin that his announced topic, "The Taste of Sin," was followed immediately by "Sweeter As the Years Go By!"

Once, just prior to addressing a group of clergymen on this subject, the writer handed a Bible to a minister on the front row and asked, "Would you read something to us for the next few minutes?" As he stared at me in mute surprise, the attention of the group became intense and electric. I reached down and took the Bible from him. "That was a rather dirty trick, wasn't it?" I asked. "Yet, how many of you have been guilty of asking your music director or song leader 'to lead a few hymns until our speaker gets here!' "

The writer has been asked upon so many occasions—without previous warning — "Mr. Thayer, would you lead us in a few hymns before we begin our meeting?" that he has adopted the practice upon entering any gathering of quietly selecting from the prevailing hymnal several which would be appropriate to the subject at hand—just in case!

In a typical denominational hymnal containing 182 carefully cross-referenced topics, plus 111 sub-topics, ranging from "Activity" to "Zion" is there not applicable material for about every part of nearly any conceivable kind of service, meeting, or individual home use?

The intelligent minister today utilizes his musical leadership to assist him in formulating a balanced, effective worship unit. He and his music director sit down together to plan, select, and arrange the various segments of the service so as to achieve a definite purpose through logical and progressive steps. Such factors as proportion of less familiar or "new" hymns, vocal range, and shades of meanings of text and stanzas receive proper attention.

Where does the lay committeeman come in? He "lengthens the right arm" of the music director in bringing information to every group in the church concerning selection of suitable and appropriate hymns for the specific occasion.

Thus we see that the hymn has a carefully planned purpose in our worship. It is not a relief agent to allow us to stand up and stretch between periods of sitting! It is not an accompaniment to scurrying late-comers. It is not a stopgap to pacify the audience while waiting for a tardy speaker. It is your chance to participate actively in the service from the depths of your soul!

You do not have to be a Caruso or a Jeannette McDonald to sing your hymns. I am convinced that the Lord listens far more sympathetically to the untrained voice that comes directly from the heart than He does to the operatic professional whose sole interest is in personal glory of volume or beauty of tone! So what if you do drop a few notes of the new hymn under the pew

Congregational Singing

the first time through? If you and I were perfect, would we have need for the church anyhow?

When your pastor and music director choose "new" hymns, what is your reaction? When a new hymn comes up, listen as the organist plays it through, take a deep breath, and go to it! Remember, even those hymns you now love best were once "new" ones. Many things you like now failed to impress you at first. It is just possible that this "something new" could enrich your life to a degree you cannot now envision! All of us have had the experience of developing warm friends from new acquaintances. You will find this to be true over and over again as you look with new eyes at your own hymnal. The perfect hymnal, like the perfect house, has not yet been assembled or built. The song which may not appeal much to you may be intimately connected with the conversion or similar experience of your neighbor. Isn't it neighborly to sing that one as lustily as you'd like to have him join you on the one your mother taught you?

The songs in our hymnals have been selected not only by musicians and ministers, thoroughly dedicated and of high repute in their fields, but by lay men and women who have taken the time and trouble to express their preferences. With 500-odd from which to choose, every member of the congregation can find many which he will come to like, and which will come to mean something special to him.

Now, why are we going into such detail about the congregational hymns? Your music director certainly is familiar with all these facts, and he is striving constantly to increase both the number with which your worshipers are familiar, and the degree of understanding with which your singers use them.

You who are privileged to represent and work with congregational singing on the music committee with your music director have one of the most important and sensitive jobs in your church! You will doubtless need a sub-committee of your own, reaching into the women's auxiliary, the men's groups, and the young people's organizations.

While your director is supplying the class of song leaders with technical training and musical know-how, you can help by seeing that the class gets the fascinating background of the hymns they are going to use. What kind of person the writer was; who the composer was; under what circumstances the words and tune were brought together; of what significance it is to us today—your director can add to this list of interesting topics to be studied!

He will gladly help you discover the rich sources of information about your hymns. Perhaps it will be the official companion volume of material to your denominational hymnal, for example. Many excellent volumes are in print on those hymns most-loved and most-sung, and upon the history and trends in our church's eventful and often turbulent history. A number of these will be found listed in the Appendix of this volume.

Probably your biggest assignment will be the helping to bring to your adult congregation an active, singing appreciation of the finest of our hymn literature.

You will soon encounter headlong that individual whose musical vocabulary is restricted to a half-dozen or less of the "good old" songs and who at first vigorously resists any attempt to increase his scope of acquaintance with new hymns.

"Let's sing a good old hymn!"

With this popular thought I am in complete accord. Do we agree, though, on what is "good," and what is "old"? First of all, is the theology expressed consistent with our beliefs today? In the era of the stern, vengeful, and ever-punishing God, with but a handful of mortals even hopeful of salvation among the multitudes eternally condemned, the following stanza appeared in one of the three hundred hymns gathered by Benjamin Keach and published in 1691 as "Spiritual Melody":

> "Here meets them now the worm that gnaws,
>   And plucks their vitals out;
> The pit, too, on them shuts her jaws!
>   This dreadful is, no doubt!"

How many young people would be inspired by another of the same era? This one was written "expressly for the young":

> "There is a dreadful Hell
>   And everlasting pains;

> There sinners must with devils dwell
> In darkness, fire, and chains.
> Can such a wretch as I
> Escape this cursed end?
> And may I hope, whene'er I die,
> I shall to heaven ascend?"

When man began to think of God as a loving Father, the songs of praise and devotion changed to fit the basic concepts. Many beautiful and inspiring hymns found their way into the hymnals. Contrast, for example, the following one with those above:

> "Father, whose everlasting love
> Thy only Son for sinners gave,
> Whose grace to all did freely move,
> And sent Him down a world to save.
>
> Help us Thy mercy to extol,
> Immense, unfathomed, unconfirmed
> To praise the Lamb who died for all,
> The general Savior for mankind!" *

Every age has had its "don't changers" as well as its pioneers, in hymnology as in other fields. As the ultraconservatives had earlier bitterly opposed the use of anything except "Psalm arrangements" for worship, so has an element in each generation protested any change. Had it not been for dedicated and competent musical leadership to seek out and preserve the best in the field, and at the same time new and challenging materials, one can shudder to think what still might be the content of our hymnals!

When our friend said "old" he meant "familiar to him" didn't he? Actually many of those to whom some of our folks cling are much more recent than the genuine classics.

"What is a 'good hymn'?" The answers to this question put to a series of individuals are quite likely to boil down to this: "The ones I know!" Many of the same individuals will view

---

* The above quotations are from *Hymns in Christian Worship* by H. A. L. Jefferson, and are used by kind permission of publishers Barrie and Rockcliff of London, England.

"new" or unknown ones, regardless of origin, quality, or composition with attitudes ranging all the way from hesitant acceptance to downright stubborn resistance. The same folks who would be up in arms if the minister preached on the same text two or three Sundays in a row will cling to a familiar few hymns week after week if they are allowed to do so!

Since all of us, to a greater or lesser degree, tend to feel more comfortable with familiar procedures and objects, is this not all the more reason to expose our adults and young people to the best in hymn literature until they make it their own?

One has but to visit a church whose music program over a period of years has made this a primary objective to hear music which is truly worthy of a part in the worship service.

The twentieth century has seen the market flooded with "collections" of "Your Favorite Hymns," a few, good — many, extremely cheap and trashy. As in any field, the church and church music are unfortunately not free from charlatans and those who would capitalize on sensationalism and cheap emotionalism. True evangelism and a program of *thoughtful revival of spiritual awareness have utilized many of the fine old, and some new gospel songs.* On the other hand, the starkly emotional rabble rousers have exploited the cheapest in text and tune to gain a few dollars in publications. "How do I tell, then," you ask, "whether a hymn is a good one or not?" Since a hymn is made of two principal ingredients, the text, or words, and a tune (with its harmonizations), it may be helpful to consider first of all each by itself, and then together, to determine the beauty and effectiveness of the "wedding" of the two.

The Hymn Text

In evaluating the text get away by yourself and read the poem aloud without music. What are the thoughts, the concepts, the total inspiration or comfort they bring you? Do they make good sense, or are they shallow doggerel?

"Bouncing to Beulahland" is somewhat incongruous to reconcile with the strength, majesty, and dignity of an all-seeing God, is it not? Do the idioms make sense today, and are the theological

Congregational Singing

concepts honest in their portrayal? If the poem really does something for you; if it lifts and inspires you, then make a mark for it on the credit side.

The Tune

Now let us listen to the tune or melody of our hymn. First of all, is the general flow of the tune in keeping with our concept of the majesty, dignity, magnitude and power of our Creator?

From your acquaintance with the personality of Jesus, how many of the tunes you know about Him would you actually be proud to sing before Him? Could you honestly meet His direct gaze and sing some of the jiggly, jouncy, "ump-ti-ump-ti-ump" stuff which has been written in the name of worship?

"Standing on the Promises" has a loping gait which suggests more dancing than solid standing! Isn't it something of a shame to wed a beautiful poem to a mere fancy-tickling tune that belongs in "Tin Pan Alley"? Compared with the dignity and four-square construction of "Stand Up, Stand Up for Jesus," the former tune suffers much!

"Oh, but," you say, "shouldn't we include some lively music in our church singing?" By all means. Such hymns as "Joyful, Joyful, We Adore Thee" set to "Ode to Joy" can hardly be surpassed in this category. There is nothing stodgy about "Praise to the Lord, the Almighty, the King of Creation," either, and this goes back to 1668—a genuine old-timer, by the way. "Onward, Christian Soldiers" certainly bespeaks the live, militant united action which must be ours today if Christianity is to survive the onslaught of Communism and corruption.

Our greatest hymns have the vibrant pulse of life and clearly defined rhythm, whether they be of the adoration and praise type, or of the classification of quiet, prayerful meditation. Avoidance of continual use of the dotted eighth and sixteenth notes, or syncopation or the oft-repeated quarter and eighth notes in six-eight measure helps to prevent sinking from the truly sublime to the ridiculous.

Melody-wise, lasting tunes usually are built on chord progressions or lines and scale sequences. Excessive use of chromatics, either melodically or chord-wise, can make a hymn too sugary or "drippy."

In this field, as in any other, a meager sampling of a few songs scarcely forms an adequate basis for judgment of what is good and worthwhile. Here, truly, "a little knowledge is a dangerous thing."

Conversely, a lively curiosity to explore and a continuing study will aid immeasurably in the formation of a basis for comparative evaluation. That hymnal of yours contains beauty and inspiration you have not yet tapped, and as for recorded music from the pens and hearts of dedicated composers, our lifetimes are not long enough to encompass all of it.

Adaptations

The adaptation of hymn poems to tunes well-known in another field is often hazardous. Not long ago the writer was asked to review a "new" collection which included an Easter poem set to the tune of "Carry Me Back to Old Virginny." Our associations with the original of this melody are so deeply set as to put to naught what the adapter hoped to accomplish. It cannot be denied, however, that many of our hymns were originally adapted from songs and music in other fields. The general character of both words and music and the continued association with some phase of worship have over a period brought about general acceptance.

One example of a beautiful adaptation is the "Prayer" taken from "Hansel and Gretel." This selection remains in its original context. Its simplicity and pure beauty and its use in the original opera give it a deserved place in our accepted and loved sacred music.

Space does not permit considerations of the vast store of interesting facts about our hymns. Only a few high spots have been touched—enough, perhaps, to prod your curiosity into some additional study. (See the Bibliography in the Appendix.)

The hymn is your part of the worship. The manner in which you sing it, or don't, usually indicates pretty accurately the amount you are putting into, or getting out of, the whole service. You know we can't sit back and dare the minister to pour salvation into us without some help!

Study your hymns by yourself. Try to catch the full meaning which the author and composer tried to convey. Then when you come to sing on Sunday morning you just may be surprised to discover how much more the organ music, the choir anthem, the spoken message, the hymn—the complete worship experience—can mean to you.

Your director will gladly help you outline class study projects on this subject for your church groups.

General Hymn Tastes

What do we do if many of our adults have been brought up on hymns some of which are under par, either musically or theologically? Well, we have to lead our people gradually from where they are to where we want them to be.

I believe that a hymn which has a deep association with an early religious experience of an individual has definite worth to him, and I'll sing it wholeheartedly with him. On the next one, though, I'll expect him to exercise mutual respect and join me just as lustily in one of my choice. I have found by experience that with a little guidance he will do just that!

You will observe your director using this technique time after time as he guides the tastes of the worshipers slowly and considerately toward richer and more meaningful musical experiences.

I sincerely believe it is our responsibility to see that the present religious experiences of our people are tied in with the best music we can put before them. This involves leading them to like it. It does not mean cramming it down their throats. Can we not make some forward progress while keeping a healthy touch with the past? The best of it, that is.

Do we not try to guide and cultivate the tastes of our people in just about every field? Why not in the music of their worship? How different is this work from that of our pastor as he labors with the attitude of heart, pattern of behavior, and strength of conviction of the flock?

Gospel vs. Classic Hymns

As for "gospel" versus "classic" hymns, why cannot the best of both live together in the same hymnal and be enjoyed by the same folks? Do they not complement each other? Let's turn for a moment to an organization to whom the gospel song is a principal tool.

Tedd Smith, pianist with Billy Graham since 1950, in his article in the November, 1960, *Decision* magazine says, "—so many of us have neglected to educate ourselves to the more serious religious music and therefore our balance in sacred music is out of proportion." And again quoting, "I wonder how many of us realize what a tremendous spiritual impact so many of the religious classics, as well as the solid gospel songs, can have on our lives?" *

What are some of the "classics" among the hymns? Here are a few: "Fairest Lord Jesus," "O God Our Help in Ages Past," "Now Thank We All Our God," "A Mighty Fortress Is Our God," "When Morning Gilds the Skies," "A Charge to Keep I Have," "Joyful, Joyful We Adore Thee," "Holy, Holy, Holy."

These are but samples of the many which comprise the truly great hymn literature of today. As more and more of our churches are making use of this quality of hymn today, we see more of our laymen working quietly side by side with their music leadership to encourage all worshipers to venture into the unknown and at first somewhat feared realm of "new hymns"!

How Meaningful Are Your Hymns?

Has your pastor ever stopped your congregation after singing a stanza of a hymn and asked, "Now what was that thought you just sang?" Did you have to bootleg a quick glance back over the words because you had been repeating mechanically some long-familiar phrases totally without thought of what they meant?

When certain stanzas have been carefully selected by your minister and music director to fit the continuity of the worship, did you sing them with serious thought or did you chafe a bit

---

* Permission to use the above quotations has been graciously granted by the Editorial Staff of *Decision*.

inwardly because someone had disturbed the accustomed flow of habit?

Let's not forget that originally many of our hymns had from twelve to sixteen stanzas. The standard "Jerusalem, My Happy Home," which now appears usually in not more than six stanzas, was originally printed in no less than twenty-six, we are told! Imagine a congregation accepting one of this length today! Around 1616, the probable time for its authorship, the two- and three-hour sermons were no novelty, either!

Singing the Phrasing

Do you sing:

"God is love; His mercy brightens [breath]
All the path in which we rove"

or

"God is love; [breath] His mercy
brightens All the path in which we rove"?

Again, in "This Is My Father's World," do you parrot:

"All nature sings, and round me rings [breath]
The music of the spheres."

or *really* sing:

"All nature sings, [breath] and round
me rings The music of the spheres!"?

"Oh, but I don't *need* a breath back there!" you say. Of course you don't, but do you always run out of gas in your tank before putting in more? When you read poetry you surely do not pause at the end of a line unless the thought and punctuation so indicate. Why sing your musical poems in a singsong, unintelligent manner? We never should break between a subject and its verb, or between a verb and its object, should we? Let's *think* as we sing!

Accompanying the Hymn

This brings us squarely to the problem of playing the organ or piano for hymn singing. Most piano teachers understand the different technique required for this work, but one snorted rather huffily, "I teach my pupils to play the notes and they can read anything!"

The accompanist who "plays the notes" of the hymn without regard to phrasing or word meaning illustrated above has much to learn in this field. The slipshod, slam-bang running through hymns in some services is anything but conducive to reverence or worship.

One day I asked a young man to play through the third stanza of "In the Hour of Trial." He looked at me in bewilderment and finally blurted, "Isn't that just like any other stanza?" We then compared the opening lines of the first and third stanzas.

(1) "In the hour of trial, Jesus, plead for me," with the breath, for untrained singers, at least, coming after two measures, or the word "trial." If we breathe or phrase in the same spot for each of the stanzas, we get in (3) "Should Thy mercy send me [pause]" we leave "Sorrow, toil, and woe" dangling out by itself. Surely the mercy is not meant to "send me!"

When the young man realized that his support of carrying the phrase, "Should Thy mercy send me Sorrow," etc., with the tiny pauses before "toil," and "woe" made a meaningful message, it was like the opening of a new world to him. "We really have to know what they are singing about, don't we?" he smiled. Would that this light might break for *all* our accompanists!

Word Emphasis

Remaining with this hymn for a moment, do you sing, or permit "IN – THE – HOUR – OF – TRI – AL" with a bing, bang, biff, swat—full force on every syllable, regardless, or do you actually *pray* it the way you would read it: "in – the – HOUR – of – TRI – al, JE – sus, – PLEAD for – ME!" Surely we let up on the less important articles, prepositions and conjunctions, plus the subordinate syllables of our words, in order to give more emphasis to the significant words.

In some of the less well-arranged hymns we discover an "of" or a "the" or an "and" on a normally strongly accented musical beat. In this case it is only common sense to emphasize the important word on the weaker beat and retain the message intended by the author.

An accompanist who deserves the name is alert to these and

other basic factors. His playing is to the hymn what a frame is to a picture. His intelligent support enhances the beauty born first in the hearts of the author and composer and presently being re-created in the lives of his singers. On the contrary, unthinking plowing through chord after chord has the same effect as daubing a brushful of whitewash down over a painstakingly executed pastel canvas.

The Hymn Is for You

All our discussion of hymns has been just for you—and me—for the folks who love to sing them. Of course our choirs might pay a bit of attention, too. After all, isn't it one of their obligations to show us the way in the telling presentation to God of this most moving church music?

How do we go about helping our director improve the quality and quantity of our church's singing? Obviously the worship hour is the time when the hymns should be sung in their entire beauty and meaning without stopping or interrupting for teaching. Some analysis, comment, or on-the-spot study is appropriate if the hymn's message is a part of the sermon, or if the latter specifically concerns the song, but schooling the congregation should be accomplished outside the formal worship hour.

The hymn singing at the more informal evening worship is an excellent place for learning new hymns. From the group of three or four often sung at the beginning of the hour, *one* may be selected for emphasis. A *brief* story about the author, composer, and hymn itself, an occasion on which it was used effectively or startlingly, any points of interest may be presented. Brevity is to be emphasized. Keep your congregation's interest.

Resist the temptation to tell about two or three songs in one evening or at any one session. Nowhere is the old adage more applicable—to keep your folks wanting just a little more!

The hymns sung at church suppers, circle meetings, men's clubs and other similar affairs offer excellent channels for training. The more intimate and less formal atmosphere here not only makes the members more at ease and receptive to study—it even invites questions about the songs! Your director may well call on you to help in looking up and presenting this fascinating kind of information. One warning, however: you may find the first stages of this study so compelling you will hate to give it up!

Your director may also use the hymn-of-the-month plan, whereby a new hymn is first played for the listeners by the organ as a part of its worship hour music. Then the choir may sing it as an anthem. After several hearings the congregation finds it to be less than a "stranger," and is ready to try to sing it themselves.

CHAPTER 12

ASSISTANCE IN THE CHURCH SCHOOL

In the duties of assisting the church school superintendent and teachers with music for devotional exercises and for correlation with the regular lesson, the music director will need at least one additional person on his committee. This person should be a singer, preferably one who can also play the piano, and who perhaps can lead some singing, herself/himself.

Each group which gathers for devotional exercises needs at least one person who is a qualified song leader plus one who can play well enough to accompany the singing. This committeeman helps find an additional pianist and/or song leader in one of the older classes to function for a younger group. He is notified of forthcoming absences and attempts to provide substitutes.

He ferrets out the boys and girls who are taking piano lessons, encourages them in their progress, and assures them they are needed to play for hymns as soon as they are able. Their piano teachers are encouraged to teach hymn-playing as soon as and as thoroughly as possible. They are recognized as being bona fide members of the music department, and receive recognition at the annual choir recognition and dedication exercises.

It is an assured fact that the young pianist is far less likely to go through the "great American ritual of dropping his music" when he is assured that there is a strong and real need for him and his playing.

We have always been careful to include not only our active accompanists for each group on "choir dedication" Sunday in the fall, but also a separate group consisting of all those who had progressed far enough in their piano lessons to play a hymn. Such public recognition may appear to be a small thing, but it can be one more incentive to encourage much-needed future accompanists to stay with their instruments.

The listing of the names of the song leaders and accompanists with the officers of each class should be assured by the committee member. A current list, something like the following, will help the director when he gathers the group to teach them (and thence to their classes) the "hymn of the month."

Church School Music Leaders		
Class	Song Leader	Accompanist

CHAPTER 13

TRAINING CLASSES

Song Leaders and Accompanists

The church which is really building for the future will plan to arrange for enough of the time of its music director to be used to teach song leaders from its own congregation. Any adult or young person who can himself sing and read music is eligible for such training. Some experience on the piano is highly desirable, but not absolutely necessary.

Junior high school age students take to such leadership like ducks to water. They can then lead the singing in their own and younger grade meetings. The senior high school student frequently develops to the point where he can lead his own age group in its Sunday morning anthems from time to time. Those young pianists who have been working toward accompanying now get their early experience in playing for the hymns and fellowship songs. How often does the church have an "all-youth program" where the organist and music director have to be the regular adults, with the rest coming from the youth ranks?

Where youth are encouraged, taught, and supervised in a systematic manner, there is much more singing and playing throughout all of the church activities. The director does the instructing and supervises at least the early experience in leading singing, but his committeeman helps others become interested, and reminds the outside piano teachers of their privileges and responsibilities in teaching hymn playing and accompanying.

Men's clubs, women's auxiliary meetings, suppers of the church, all wish to have leaders who can "make things go" and pianists who can accompany well. Even in larger churches which have been supporting such leadership training for some years, the writer has never found a superabundance of either song leaders or accompanists.

Many adults with adequate musical background will, with a little nudging, also prepare themselves for such leadership. Those who are advanced are invaluable in assisting with the sectional rehearsals of the adult choir on learning parts.

The music director is, of course, directly responsible, but much of his time is freed for musical things when the committeeman can accomplish many of the non-musical details. By this means a number of young people have been started on successful careers in music. Talent is exposed and encouraged which otherwise might never have been discovered.

Use of the Organ

As young pianists develop, many of them will want to, and should be encouraged to embark on the exciting career of playing the organ. The church-wide policy of the use of the organ will be treated more in detail later, but for its own serious and careful people, the furnishing of the church instrument without charge is but clear, common sense. Do we exact a fee from each churchgoer for walking on the aisle carpet? Is there an individual charge for weekly use of the hymnal? Is there a per capita tax for the lights used at the young people's meeting?

Surely, the use of the organ is coming up for discussion. The organ is going to wear out, as is any other piece of equipment. Manufacturers agree that the regularly and often-used instrument stays in better condition far longer than one which undergoes long periods of disuse.

The "training" committeeman may be responsible for maintaining regular schedules of practice and use of the organ, as well as executing the policy for "outside use" agreed upon by the church authorities. Again, these are important but time-consuming details which the music director is glad to delegate to his trusted co-workers.

The supervised use of the organ is customarily made available to qualified members of the congregation for lessons and practice. Requests are frequently received from organists and students outside for use of the instrument, however, and a policy for either granting or refusing such permission must be adopted.

In a number of instances a nominal charge is made for that outside use where there are free hours on the instrument, and the money goes into the organ maintenance fund. At the first sign of neglect or misuse by *anyone,* family or outsider, further privilege of the instrument is promptly denied to that person.

Music Reading

Where elementary music reading classes can be included, both adults and young people are sure to take advantage of them. Here again, a surprising number of grown-ups, even middle-aged and older, are eager to learn to do something "I've always wanted to do!" Just in casual conversations and "noising about" the information about such classes the layman can and does reach many who otherwise would not be reached by the director.

Here, too, keeping records on the attendance and other mechanical details gives the much-desired status and attention which will in turn attract and serve more people from the congregation.

Certificates

Certificates of recognition for completion of such courses in music reading, song leading, and accompanying are of unquestionable value and encouragement. Many adults will at first outwardly pooh-pooh the idea, but the writer has never found a person who refused to accept the certificate with his name on it! This committee "training leader" may well be delegated by the music leader to make the public awards at the chosen time.

Classes Worthwhile?

Through the offering of these music reading classes for adults "starting from scratch," the writer has helped uncounted scores of men and women to self-satisfying participation in singing the beloved hymns of their churches. Grown-up after grown-up who was told as a child, "Aw, you can't sing!" by an older brother or sister; or, "You just listen while the rest of the class sings!" by an insufficiently informed grade school music teacher, discovers under sympathetic guidance that he *can sing!*

After years of mute and yearning silence in the midst of others long thought to be "more talented," these people now lift their own voices in joyful expression of personal worship.

Each semester in college, in teaching "Music Activities for the Classroom Teacher" to adults who are required to include this three hours of credit for an all-levels teaching certificate or for a degree, the writer finds many adults who have feared and postponed this particular course because they "can't sing." Each semester the same drama unfolds: always old, yet ever new with the thrill of one's personal discovery of his God-given voice!

All it takes is patient working with muscles and mental coordination long unused. Can there be any greater reward than to hear, "Mr. Thayer, I can sing in church now, and the tune comes out right!" Time and again comes the declaration, "If I never got one other thing out of this course, the knowing that I can sing is worth far more than I have ever spent on *any* training in my life!"

Are such adult training classes worthwhile in *your* church? Might the above be the reason why some of your people passively hold their hymnals and seem not to be as much a part of the drama of worship as you would like?

CHAPTER 14

SPECIAL SERVICES AND PROGRAMS

Special services and programs require additional preparation and careful attention to production details if these functions are to proceed smoothly. Often less than the full impact desired for a program may be achieved because projection equipment or other vital machinery has not been properly checked well in advance.

Confusion and lack of adequate seating for a multiple choir service may result when ushers have not been properly instructed. The author has occasionally encountered half-kidding but half-serious protestations from adults when he has insisted that they actually attend and physically "walk through" the procedures at a rehearsal for a forthcoming program. These same good people, however, have been most appreciative of this preparation when the whole affair is successfully culminated.

The thoughtful music director is *always careful* to include even the third assistant door opener in his acknowledgments when the program is over.

Sometimes we forget to notify our custodian of a special event until the day before—or even the morning of the fateful evening. Should we be astonished if he is somewhat less than happy about the whole thing? Should we be disappointed when he fails to drop everything and jump wholeheartedly to help us? No, the man without whom we could not even function should be advised of all special plans even before, or as soon as they appear on the church calendar. I would go so far as to make sure he has a copy of the whole year's program as soon as it is decided upon, for he is an essential member of the team.

And how do we approach him when we need something? "We have to have a supplementary platform built out from the pulpit to take care of the orchestra!" Such a pre-emptory demand is often met with unspoken resentment, if not open hostility by an already overworked custodian. I have found the following approach to be most successful in such a situation. "Mr. Conrad, I need some advice on a problem. Can you help me?" Then as we stand before the pulpit, I continue, "Now the choir takes up this much room. The orchestra we'd like to have will come to about here. What would you suggest?" "Well, a temporary platform to here should take care of the situation." What a difference when he feels he has a part in decisions and planning for these occasions!

Consideration for the other fellow's pride and feeling of being a part of the team always pays rich dividends to him who remembers to use it.

He is complimented when he is approached for advice. His suggestions frequently prove to be invaluable in helping to smooth out many small problems. A small detail has a way of assuming proportions sufficient to ruin the timing or the sustained train of thought of a service when neglected.

Check Sheet

The following outline is presented as a method of double-checking some of the many details involved in any program outside the routine worship service. While each director and committee will doubtless wish to set up similar ones to fit individual needs, this one has served well on many occasions. It has been adapted for the music department from a general one originally provided for his staff by Dr. Ralph H. Seiler, pastor of the Asbury

Special Services and Programs 107

Methodist Church of El Paso when the author was minister of music there. For the sake of brevity the explanatory notes may be omitted.

Services and Programs—Check Sheet

Occasion_____ Date_____ Day_____ Hour_____
Cleared with office_____ On church calendar_____
               (date)   (date)
Space needed_____
                (rooms, buildings, outside areas)
Groups participating_____
Leaders involved_____
Dates notified_____
Custodian notified_____
            (date)
Subject matter or music required_____
_____
Costumes, robes, or other dress_____
Reference materials_____
        (such as books on authenticity of period, etc.)
Requirements: chairs_____ tables_____ heat_____ pews_____
              projection_____ lighting_____
              other _____
Director's facilities: stand_____ light_____ program mat._____
Instructions to participants: rehearsals_____
  extra rehearsals_____
  time to arrive for program_____ location to report_____
  parent cooperation needed_____
  special instructions_____
Accompanists _____
Librarians_____ Properties_____
Ushers _____
  Notified by_____ Date_____
  Special instructions_____
Dressing of altar, or other instructions_____
Public relations: publicity_____ Notified_____
                    (person)   (date)

newspapers_____ church papers_____
church bulletin_____ radio_____ posters_____
TV_____ bulletin boards_____ others_____
Program_____ dates to be printed_____
    (person responsible)
date submitted for printing_____ proof-read_____
Nursery needed_____ from_____to_____
                                    (hour)   (hour)
Arrangements for nursery made_____ date_____
Final review of program with key personnel_____
    (Check **all** facilities and personnel.)

* * * * *

Cleaning Up and Returning Equipment After Program

Cleaning up, replacing furniture, and returning borrowed equipment afterward is an essential part of each program. Definite planning and definite assignment of duties here is as necessary as for any part of the participation.

The writer has often used the following cards to reinforce his less-than-perfect memory for checking the integral details of a large program. (Probably *you* won't need them, but I'll print it, anyhow!)

Time and date_____
No. of key(s) checked out_____
Eqpt. chkd. out or to be used_____

Persons responsible_____
How long property will be needed_____
Person lending eqpt._____
Returned_____ Thanked_____

Special Services and Programs

Ah, how blessed is he who returns promptly that which he has borrowed! Truly, now, if we have time to go *borrow* something, have we not also time to return it after we have used it?

(3"x5")
Job Assignment
Job: _____
To be completed by_____
   (date)
Person assigned:_____
Notified:_____
Completed:_____

CHAPTER 15

MASSED GROUP FESTIVALS
AND COMPETITIONS

Improved communications and faster transportation have done much to encourage the current trend of church choir festivals and competitions. Several denominations now conduct annual contests in which soloists and ensembles of all sizes are evaluated either against each other or against accepted standards of excellence.

Churches of different denominations are, upon occasion, combining their efforts in concerted praise to God, showing that all of us *can* work together.

Both the festival and competition movements are extremely beneficial when properly run, and should be encouraged by every possible means. Participation in either entails much planning and work by many people in addition to the music director.

On some occasions, especially during the fast-growing summer camp and retreat projects the church music department conducts joint projects with the youth department or other units of the church.

For some years it was the privilege of this writer to serve as executive secretary of the Pennsylvania Forensic and Music League. This organization, sponsored by the Extension Division of the University of Pittsburgh, conducted state-wide competitions in more than eighty different events in music and speech in the high schools of Pennsylvania.

Twenty-odd committees were required to insure smooth operation of these competition-festivals. This same kind of organization, on a more modified scale, has helped to make successful many choir festivals and programs involving large groups of people and many out of town visitors.

These committees and their assignments are presented in the following pages together with comments and suggested implementation. The active church will find the use of at least some of these committees to be valuable in planning its activities.

HOUSING

    Securing housing for students
    Individual homes
    Coordinating work with registration committee
    Keep registration information up-to-date for emergency calls from people's homes
    Dormitory (or home) arrangements
    Hotel reservations for judges, chairmen, and other officials

*   *   *   *   *

When Asbury Church was privileged to have the McMurry College Choir under the direction of Dr. Richard von Ende for a guest appearance the procedure followed will illustrate. Well in advance of the concert date it was learned that eighteen men and twenty women would be coming to El Paso. Our congregation was apprised of the need for entertaining these young people in homes. The cards on the following page were passed out and duly completed.

These records were also useful for our church "Thank you" cards after the program.

Be sure that the director, accompanist, and bus drivers are included in housing assignments. (However, bus companies often provide for the driver.)

About two weeks before the program, upon receipt of the names list by men and by women, assignments were made and hosts were notified as to sex and number of guests, and probable arrival hour. The following cards were then completed *in duplicate:*

McMurry College Choir Concert

Housing

Name_____ Address_____
Phone_____

I shall be glad to provide room for _____ students for the night of February 27th.
I can/cannot provide transportation to and from church.
I prefer men/women (circle one).
I will/cannot furnish breakfast for these students.

- -

(office use)
Students assigned:
    men   women

_____   _____
_____   _____

Date_____ Assigned by_____

Host Card—McMurry Chanters
for Feb. 27, 19____

Chorister _____
Host _____
  Address _____
  Telephone _____
Asbury Methodist Church, 3500 Hueco
Tel. 565-2801

By the scheduled arrival hour the host committee had the cards arranged at a long table in the Community Hall.

Hosts with their cars, and several extra drivers with cars for the homes which could not furnish transportation were also waiting. As a guest received his copy of the card, the host name was called, the driver introduced, and the singer was on his way. It will be noted that the cards carried the church address and telephone as well as those of the host. We were later told that students used these cards to address "thank-you" notes after their visit.

The second card was kept in the file at church. The office phone was staffed until midnight and then at an early hour next morning. Unnecessary precaution? Just before supper a long distance call notified us that the father of one of the boys had just sustained a severe heart attack. Within minutes the boy and Dr. von Ende were called, and the boy was en route to the airport and home.

MEALS

Ascertain resources of restaurants in area
Hours at which visitors can best be served
Arrange menus
Obtain contracts for desired meals from visiting directors
Determine hours during which feeding facilities will be open

* * * * *

Where visiting groups wish to have arrangements made in advance for restaurant meals, it is wise to have a written agreement for financial responsibility signed in advance. On one occasion a director had asked to have seventy-six noon meals prepared. Agreements with him and the restaurant were verbal. His group performed and were through by eleven o'clock. He suddenly decided to leave town immediately and get the meal on the road. Remonstrances to him concerning his responsibility and the restaurant's loss were of no avail. The reaction of the manager was normal. While such a breach of agreement is uncommon, one example has been enough to require all future requests to be made in writing.

MEAL AGREEMENT

Organization_____ Date_____

I wish to contract for the following meals on specified dates as follows:

Date_____19__   _____breakfasts @ $_____each
                    (number)   (min. and/or max.)
                    _____noon meals @ $_____each
                    _____evening meals @ $_____each

I will be financially responsible for the meals requested above.

Signed _____
Address_____ Tel._____
Official position_____

When no definite commitments are made in advance, eating places in the vicinity should still be advised of the approximate number of visitors expected for what days.

* * * * *

Massed Group Festivals and Competitions

TREASURER
- Receive participation fees
  - (a) from individual soloists and small groups which arrive early
  - (b) from directors of large groups
- Punch eligibility cards to indicate fees paid
- For persons who have lost eligibility cards, refer to executive secretary

REGISTRATION
- Check eligibility cards against certification sheet provided by executive secretary
- Determine fees have been paid
- Check off on official certification sheet
- Distribute schedules and information sheets to registrants
- Include one complete program for each director
- Distribute identification badges
- Distribute guest car stickers

HEALTH AND SAFETY
- Locate and mark boys' and girls' rest rooms
- Establish first-aid stations or facilities at strategic locations
- Have nurses on duty at first-aid stations
- Establish twenty-four-hour schedule availability
- Have doctor available by telephone at all times

EVENTS ROOMS
- Ascertain what rooms will be needed for events as scheduled
- See that time and purpose of use of rooms is clearly understood with organizations
- See that events do not conflict in time or location (large group music events, for example, should be segregated sufficiently to prevent disturbance to solo or speech events)
- See that rooms and stage are of sufficient size for participants
- Provide sight-reading rooms for large groups (isolated from other events)
- Provide warmup rooms (where required)
- Provide floor plans of buildings and rooms where necessary

EQUIPMENT

See that rooms have proper equipment for scheduled events
Music events: pianos, chairs, stands, podium
Speech events: Table and/or platform, chairs
Pianos tuned to A=440
Risers for group rooms (where available)
Be sure all borrowed property is properly marked for identification for return
Establish responsibility for equipment with room chairman
  He must be responsible for all room contents until it is properly turned over to his successor.

BUILDINGS

This is a public relations committee designed to acquaint organizations who are asked to lend facilities for the contests, with the purpose, scope, and operation of the league. This group necessarily works very closely with the events rooms committee in providing contest locations.

HOME ROOMS

Assign headquarters for participating groups
Rooms for wraps, cases, bags
Provide guards or locks for directors
Determine from registration the size, location, or other needs of each organization
Have rooms clearly marked prior to arrival of contestants
Caution occupants about careful use of facilities provided

PUBLIC RELATIONS

Full information prior to, and during contest to be provided through the following media: papers, radio, clubs, schools, television, Chamber of Commerce
Public information must be continuous, timely, and provided to all possible media

SIGNS AND MAPS

Determine needs of committees and mark adequately for strangers, especially: events rooms, home rooms, traffic, health and safety, staging

Massed Group Festivals and Competitions

Provide map of city or of all contest area in sufficient detail to facilitate easy access to all contest sites
Provide registration committee with adequate supply
Post one such map at each contest site

BALLOTING

Provide room and two tables for balloting committee at contest headquarters
Provide following: calculating machine, two typewriters, paper, carbons
Stock supply of ballots for all events
Record and file final events
Make copy of results for (a) bulletin board, (b) newspapers

OFFICIAL CARS

Volunteer drivers and cars for duty at each contest site, for purpose of moving accompanists, ballot-carrying aides, judges, or other officials between contest locations
Two cars at general headquarters
Provide these facilities at least thirty minutes ahead of contest hours
See that official cars are provided with proper stickers

TRAFFIC AND PARKING

This committee will work closely with the police department, and will be responsible for the following items:
Space in front of each contest site for official cars
Arrange for parking area for buses
Arrange convenient area for out-of-town guest cars
See that official and guest cars and buses are provided with proper stickers
Arrange loading and unloading space for buses at home room buildings

AIDES AND MESSENGERS

Provide two messengers at each contest site to carry ballots and messages
Provide enough aides at headquarters for needed communication
Assign one student doorkeeper for each room opening of each

contest site to control entering and leaving at proper times and to collect tickets

It is extremely important that no one be allowed to interrupt any performance by entering, leaving, or otherwise disturbing during its progress. These doorkeepers must maintain proper order at all times.

Program Printing

Arrange general format and composition of official program for contest

Check proofreading and delivery to contest headquaters

Ticket and Program Distribution

Set up sales unit for each major contest site

Distribute tickets and programs to these units

Be responsible for materials and moneys

Arrange with aides and messengers committee for needed personnel

Music Staging

Arrange traffic for large group events sites

See that groups enter at one end of stage and leave at other to prevent congestion and delay

Provide two students at each band and orchestra site to assist groups with re-setting the stage. These students should themselves be older members of both band and orchestra. Provide helpers with seating charts sent in from participants

Music Events Committee

Assist general chairman in obtaining music judges, chairmen, time-keepers

See that these people are properly instructed and trained

Have extra personnel available for emergency purposes

Event Chairman, Timekeeper

Each event must have a chairman who is responsible for moving the events smoothly and on time, ascertaining that participants conform to all rules. He introduces each event and sees that proper courtesy is afforded to all. He also may be the timekeeper, or a separate person may be assigned for this duty.

VICE-CHAIRMAN

Set up general headquarters

Arrange with committees to have each committee represented at all times at headquarters

Check progress and functions of each committee

Have mimeograph facilities available for emergency announcements

Provide 1 or 2 telephones at headquarters

Provide all committees with complete lists and telephone numbers of: general headquarters, contest sites, housing locations

JUDGES AND CHAIRMEN AT CONTEST

Have judges and chairmen check in on arrival

See that chairmen receive: instructions, materials, and directions to the proper locations

Have all concerned sign and return expense vouchers

After each contest event, have chairman turn in: reports, comment rating sheets, music and materials

Make sure there is a comment rating sheet for each contestant

Return music to contestant

Before releasing judges see that all adjudication sheets are signed, and comments are complete

GENERAL ENTERTAINMENT

This committee will have general charge of whatever entertainment activities may be agreed upon in advance of the contest. They will arrange any pre-contest meeting of judges and chairmen, any scheduled party for students, and other general gatherings of this nature.

CHAPTER 16

VESTMENTS

The desirability of wearing robes by the choirs is generally accepted today. Since a number of other texts cover this subject quite fully, only the principal reasons for robing will be mentioned here.

There can be no doubt that the wearing of vestments adds to the dignity and worship atmosphere of the service. Insistence on suitable demeanor and conduct while wearing the robe is conducive to the general air of reverence of the worship hour.

Startling and sometimes clashing juxtaposition of colors and styles of clothing can be avoided by the use of uniform garb of the singers.

One of the more vital principal reasons for robes, though, is the wide range of economic status represented in the choir. Here, wealth and very limited means often stand shoulder to shoulder. The tendency to dress up for choir and competition in appearance is effectively eliminated where robes bring all members to worship in common attire.

While the lack of suitable clothing rarely is voiced as the real reason for a singer's quietly dropping out, it does happen where no robes are provided. The writer has found this to be especially true in age-group choirs, where parents are often quite sensitive about the appearance of their children in comparison with others.

In chapter 9 the duties of the robe chairman of each choir are outlined. Either the chairman or an assistant (or two) must be able to use a sewing machine to make the inevitable changes in robe lengths and to mend minor tears.

A complete and descriptive inventory of robes is the first step in this area. This "master list" of robes owned for each choir should be kept separate from the "in use" list, and changed only as robes are added or dropped when worn out.

The current list on the same form contains the same information plus the name of the person to whom issued, date of issuance, and of return. The "notes" space permits notes for such needs as replacement of a hook or repair of slide fastener. This list should be posted in the robe room in a spot easily visible to all singers.

A permanent number should be sewn into the inside of the back of the collar. The name of the current wearer should be sewn in beside the permanent number tag. This eliminates confusion on Sunday morning when the minutes are short and people forget their numbers and have to refer to the posted list, or grab the robe assigned to someone else!

A form like the following can be useful:

_____ CHURCH MINISTRY OF MUSIC

CHOIR INVENTORY SHEET Page _____ of _____ pages

_____ Choir   Date _____

Robe description (colors, components, etc.)

No.	M	F	Chest, Bust	Possible lengths	Sleeve lengths	Issued to:	Date	Ret'd	Notes:

The chairman can ascertain by a glance at the "possible lengths" column which hem can be let out to accommodate the new member. The distance from the bottom of the robe to the floor is a matter of choice of the director and choir, but six inches is both common in use and is entirely practical.

Constant liaison with membership chairman enables the robe chairman to know at a glance what robes are in use and which are available for new members. Pencil use on the "in use" list will eliminate, to a considerable degree, retyping the list.

In purchasing robes it is well to check with the manufacturer as to the surplus in the hems, both in the sleeves and bottoms of robes.

Sometimes a member who has started to grow careless in attendance can be prodded into regularity by a reminder that he cannot be allowed to tie up a robe which is needed for a new member. Prompt installation of the name in the robe and just as prompt removal of an inactive name will help to remind all that choir membership is a privilege not to be taken lightly.

While we are on the subject of robe sizes may we remind the chairman once more not to be dismayed to find in the fall that all carefully adjusted hems for the previous Easter are now "stair steps." This is especially true in the age groups. The astonishing growth of our youngsters often requires adjustment of hems as often as twice a year.

The robe chairman will keep constant watch for little tears, opened seams and faulty fastenings. Here is truly a case where "a stitch in time saves nine!" Broken stitches in a hem are at the same time unsightly and a hazard to the wearer. The last minute safety pin can cause a loop, which caught in a careless heel can cause a bad fall!

White collars, when used for the women, are usually laundered and pressed by the wearers. Boxes or drawers of extra clean ones should be on hand.

Cleaning of robes is done several times a year, and especially just before Christmas and Easter. Any robe turned in is, of course, cleaned before being used by another singer.

The robe chairman will need to instruct and remind the choir as to proper donning, doffing, and hanging of the robes. Many singers do not know, or will forget that the robe must be hung evenly on the hanger (wooden or plastic preferred) with the top hook secured if the robe is to hang without wrinkling on the rack.

By now it must be apparent that the committee on robes is a busy one!

Robe closets or robe rooms need to be located near, or adjacent to the rehearsal room. Dustproof closets will decrease cleaning expense to a measurable degree. Closet fronts should consist of a series of narrow doors, which will enable many singers to obtain their robes at the same time.

Hanging facilities should keep the robes at least three inches apart to prevent crushing or wrinkling. These same facilities are adequate for hanging outside wraps of the singers. An excellent homemade arrangement can be fashioned from a length of 1½ or 1¼ inch pipe and a piece of 1'x2' piece of lumber. After the pipe is secured in place by block brackets, the 1'x2' piece of lumber is first sawed with notches large and deep enough to admit hanger hooks and then secured above the pipe. Center the saw cuts at three inches. Seven-eighths of an inch should be deep enough to permit easy insertion of hanger hook. The space above the cuts is thus adequate for name plates.

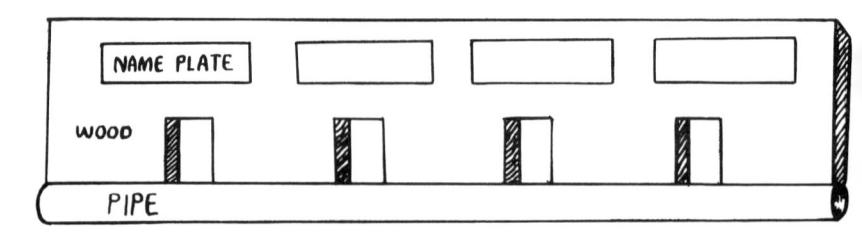

A shelf above the rack provides a place for boxes of collars. Racks on wheels, such as used in a clothing store, are an alternate means of hanging robes. The racks are covered with plastic dust hoods and wheeled into closets. At service time the racks are rolled out into the choir room where all members can obtain robes simultaneously. While considerably more expensive in first cost, this means can be counted on as a permanent investment.

The type and style of robe to be purchased will be for the director, choir, music committee, and pastor to decide. This writer believes that simplicity and dignity should be the paramount factors in this choice. Cloth weight should be as light as possible consistent with durability and wrinkle-free appearance. The current wide range of synthetic materials offers most acceptable solutions here.

Long experience indicates that the large hook and receiver fastenings are to be preferred over the slide fastener, or "zipper." The latter works well when new. After a few cleanings, however, when the original lubricant has been removed, the slides will jam quite easily. Major vestment companies offer a choice of fastenings.

Some churches find the purchase of robe "kits" to be satisfactory. Where skilled seamstresses are available in the congregation a considerable savings can be effected in first costs. Several companies offer these kits in desired sizes ready for assembling.

Many directors establish the procedure of issuing to a member a robe, hymnal, and music folder with the same number. This does add to the ease of remembering which belongs to whom!

CHAPTER 17

YOUR MUSIC ROOM

Your administration has embarked on a music program which includes a carefully chosen director and a capable organist. You envision choirs of big people and little people, and are convinced that, at last you are on your way.

What kind of place have you planned for all those people to work? Are your choirs going to sing in a room which will have as nearly as possible the same acoustic properties as your sanctuary? Is there provision for orderly, practical storage of music? Are robe closets dustproof and large enough to hang all vestments without crumpling? Is there an office where your director can administer your program and can hold uninterrupted conferences while the main room may be in full use?

Can the room be used any time, day or night, without interruption to, or from other neighboring groups? Of special interest to the choir is its warm-up period immediately preceding each service. Why a room for "warm-up" purposes on Sunday morning?

In his book, *When You Build Your Church* (Meredith Press), Dr. John R. Scotford, an internationally recognized authority on church architecture, commented, "Many, although not all choirs like to 'warm up' on Sunday morning before the service. If good work has been done at rehearsals we wonder how necessary this is . . . ."

His whole chapter on "Giving Music Its Place" testifies to his basic concern in the problems which face many of us today. The chapter ends: "Music is becoming increasingly important in Protestant churches. The physical facilities which are needed should receive far more thought than has been given them in the past. A happy choir and a contented organist are a great asset to any church." (Quotations used by kind permission of the Meredith Press.)

The writer took time to write to Dr. Scotford, submitting the following reasons for such a room:

1. No matter how well the anthems and other music were prepared at the weekly rehearsal each member has been engrossed in countless daily activities since Thursday night. A quick review is needed to insure confident and concerted interpretation of the musical and spiritual message.

2. A brief warmup of vocal and muscular "machinery" is as necessary to the singer as the warm-up throws of a baseball pitcher in the bull pen.

3. Most important of all is the establishment of the atmosphere of worship in the choir. "Did I turn off the heat under the roast?" "Did Eveline pick up her offering envelope?" "I must go over that business trip outline again this afternoon!" All these thoughts must be erased, and minds and hearts united through the quiet prayer and meditation which precedes the entrance to the choir loft.

Dr. Scotford most graciously replied, "This is the first time any music director has taken the trouble to explain these needs to me. In the future I will be better prepared to help our music people get the facilities they need."

While competent church architects of today are aware of modern choir training needs and will recommend adequate practice facilities accordingly, there still exist those bid-hungry or just plain ignorant individuals who will lie, "Oh, your choirs can use any of these classrooms and you can save a lot of money!"

They proceed to label as "Choir Room" a 6x9 closet which is too small for *any* choir purpose except perhaps its library. Exaggeration? The reader need not travel far to observe such impossible conditions in existence.

What if your present plant suffers from such a lack of planning? Obviously a revision of some existing room(s) or the addition of suitable quarters is indicated. First of all, from our ever-present measuring stick of economy, how much use will such a room get? This may come as a surprise to many, but in a church with a full-fledged program of age-group choirs no area *but the full-time church office* will be utilized more! Furthermore the independent heating/cooling facilities and the superior lighting of this room are bound to be popular for meetings of other church groups on the infrequent occasions when choirs, ensembles, or soloists are not in operation.

Exact dimensions of rooms will, for the most part, be intentionally avoided in this chapter, although space requirements will be stated in formula form. The definite needs will be pointed up. Measurements for adequate facilities must follow careful planning for one, two, five years ahead by pastor, director, and committee. Heavy reliance must lie on your director, for he is the one from whom you expect effective results. Can you do less than provide him with means of getting the job done?

Separate control valves to central heating and cooling systems or independent units for this area have been proved to be most economical. In modern building it is fortunately no longer necessary to heat large areas of the plant when only a room or two will be in use.

Your music groups which are expected to be fully prepared and ready for services *each week* must be provided suitable areas and facilities for the work they need to do. They will need your protection, too, from encroachment of other of the church groups on the allotted periods and rooms for rehearsals.

Reasons for not using the sanctuary for choir rehearsals are numerous and potent ones. It is economically wasteful to heat or cool such a large cubage for the comparatively small group. When the sanctuary is required for a wedding or other meeting, the choir on whose night the function falls is disabled for that evening, and thus hurt for the following Sunday.

A sanctuary rehearsal requires all music and equipment to be hauled to and from the spot—much unnecessary effort.

Your trained director knows the piano is far superior to the organ for practice sessions. The organ obscures too many mistakes which can be noted quickly and corrected when the piano is used. With the latter the accompanist can temporarily intensify one singing part which may need bolstering while the singers are learning. Many sanctuaries contain the organ only.

The sanctuary has, or should have an atmosphere of worship and devotion. In preparatory stages the choir's efforts should have the complete freedom of workshop surroundings. When hymns, anthems, responses are fully prepared a brief period with the organ gives the director a means of making final adjustments of balance, voicing, registration, and volume for the final presentation.

Seating of your choirs in their practice periods should be as much like that in the sanctuary as possible. Therefore the rehearsal room needs to be this large, plus plenty of space for piano, podium, the movable music racks, and getting to and from seats. Provision of needed reverberation space and acoustical treatment of walls, floors, and ceiling to assure the desired degree of tone reflection should be worked out with your director and a sound engineer.

According to formulas arrived at over a period of many years by the Music Educators National Conference, the following is the minimum for *seating* area to be desired:

Ten square feet per person for vocal groups

Twenty square feet per person for instrumental groups

The other adjuncts in the room mentioned earlier require additional square footage. Minimum room height should be twelve feet.

The lighting in this room is extremely important because of the required simultaneous reading of musical scores and words. An intensity of fifty foot candles at reading height from the floor is highly desirable, with no glare at any point in the room.

A minimum of thirty-five foot candles is the least for workable conditions. (A proper measuring device is a light meter.)

In poorly lighted rooms in which some choirs attempt to function, singers will attend a few times, then quietly drift away. The importance of lighting as well as adequate ventilation and controlled temperature in your choir room can hardly be overemphasized. Speaking of ventilation, did you know that an active singing group uses up the oxygen in a room much more rapidly than the same group sitting quietly? Frequent change of the room's air content without disagreeable drafts is needed.

For the same reasons that attractive finishes are expected for interiors of your sanctuary, or church school rooms and offices, should not the room in which your music groups live so much of the time be cheerful and appointed with care? Light-tinted walls and ceiling will, furthermore, help make the most of your light fixtures.

Movable risers are growing in popularity. Commercial folding ones are available from a number of school music supply houses, or homemade ones may be put together at much less cost. The raising of back rows of singers aids in seeing the director, in general blend of tone, and in full utilization of each voice in the ensemble.

Sections five feet in length will hold three chairs each. A width of three feet six inches is the required minimum, with a four-foot one needed if your choir uses music stands. A six-inch height is the usual one; with eight inches sometimes being preferred. These five-foot units can be constructed easily, moved handily, and adjusted quickly. The convenience of the hand-holes in either end is worth the extra effort of making them.

Usual arrangement is to leave one row of chairs on floor level, one on the first six-inch risers, and the third on the row of the two tiers or risers. A three-sided arrangement is easily accomplished via addition of triangular sections at the ends of the back rows.

Where the back risers are not placed against the rear wall of the room, a three-quarter inch quarter round strip will prevent

Movable risers

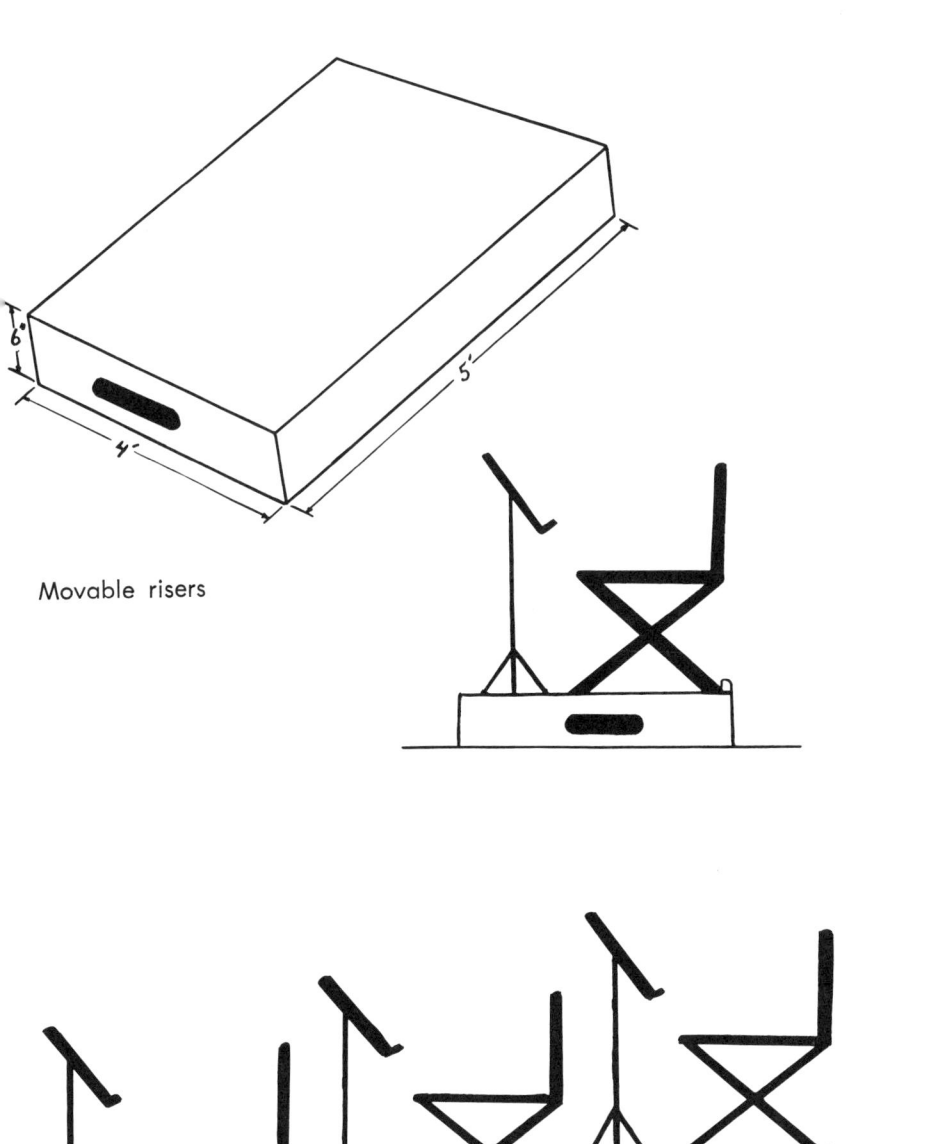

Risers in position

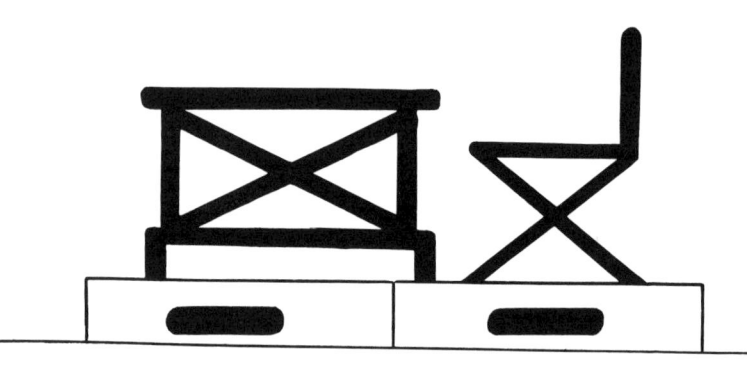

Risers used for speakers table

Hymnal rack (See page 136)

Your Music Room

the chair legs from being inadvertantly shoved backward over the edge of the risers.

It has been discovered that these risers make excellent bases for the speaker's table and chairs in the church dining room. Dramatic groups may also wish to use them for plays. Augmentation of the pulpit platform when instrumental groups accompany the choir can be accomplished.

Ends and sides are of 1" boards (actual ¾ inch). Top surface is ½" plywood (or complete riser can be made of this size plywood). If desired, 2"x2" reinforcing strips may be installed across the middle of the underside to stiffen the flooring.

Some churches build in permanent risers for a part of the choir room to copy the seating elevations in the choir loft of the sanctuary. The advantage of this construction is obvious.

One more thought on the size of your music room may be in order. While the limits of your choirs are more or less effectively prescribed by the allotted space for them in the sanctuary, you may well some day (if not now) have a flourishing orchestra which will require a greater area than your largest choir—twenty square feet per player. While normally performing on the stage or the main floor of your community hall, this group also needs an appropriate place to practice regularly, and store instruments.

In all probability all your training classes for music reading and song leaders will be held in this room. You are aware by this time, I am sure, that this will be the busiest center in your church!

One more feature which is frequently overlooked in locating the music room is placement where there is direct access from the outside without having to open other areas of the church on rehearsal night. Prowlers and other unwelcome visitors are thus prevented.

It is also most desirable to have adjacent rest rooms (which on Sunday are available to the whole church, of course).

Your new church plant planners should also place the nursery close to the music room (and *not* simply for the common purpose of sound isolation!). Furnishing of nursery accommodation definitely decides pro or con the choir participation of many

With music stands

Your Music Room

young fathers and mothers. In a number of churches served by the writer, we could not have operated our senior choirs successfully without the nursery—on rehearsal nights as well as Sundays.

A director's podium three to three and one-half feet square and from six to eight inches high should be provided so the director can be seen easily by each singer. This is especially important if risers are not used for the choir.

Without music stands

While music stands have not yet been universally adopted, choirs now using them would never give them up. Holding the music high enough so the director can be seen gets to be tiresome long before the practice is over. Stands will support music at the desired height and provide a surface for writing in the director's suggestions and score markings.

A large chalk board behind the director is indispensable. A cork-backed bulletin board near the entrance of the room is another "must."

The individually-compartmented hymnal rack just inside the door adds years to the life of the hymnals. When the director has these constantly used items numbered and makes each individual responsible for his own, everything seems to last much longer! Number and name plates above the compartments make for instant and accurate placement, finding, and checking. This is another do-it-yourself item which adds just one more reason for pride in the choir's own "home." The one illustrated is smaller than most choirs will require.

When the electric clock is placed on the wall in the back of the room, the director can easily time his carefully-planned segments of the rehearsal, and the dial will not be too handy for the few inevitable clock-watchers.

Over a period of years the investment in music itself becomes a considerable one. This good music which can, and should be used over again many times deserves careful cataloguing, numbering and storage. Both the four-drawer filing cabinet and the three-inch deep shelf boxes for octavo size are acceptable. Open piling on shelves invites dust and almost always results in sloppy, careless appearance and many "lost" selections. A small room with a door which can be locked is essential if the large music room is to be used by other groups.

Systematic issuing and returning of anthems is another essential for insuring every singer a copy and for promoting longer life to the music. A wheeled sorting rack big enough to hold *all* the cardboard folders for your choir provides instant access to all the music to be worked on for the evening. Repeated refer-

Your Music Room 137

ence is made to this kind of rack because of its importance in saving practice time.

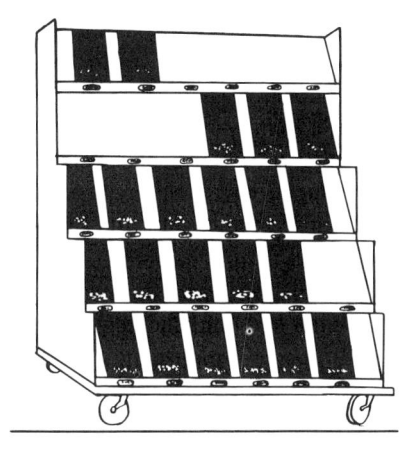

Front

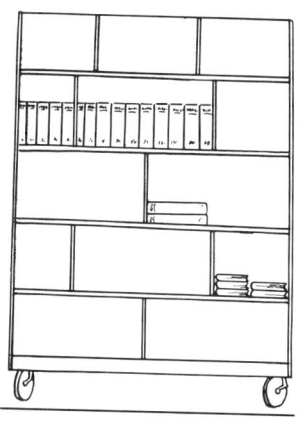

Back

The out-dated and inexcusable practice of "passing out" a number after rehearsal has begun, working on it, "passing it in," then "passing out" another is a profligate waste of time and a breeder of wandering attention and loss of interest. Often good singers will quietly leave such an ill-run group after they have been accustomed to having all of the evening's numbers in one folder and utilizing to the fullest every minute of a well-planned and executed rehearsal.

When the chorister enters the music room he picks up his hymnal from its compartment, obtains his folder (with his name and part on the front) from the rack, goes to his *assigned* seat, and *immediately* arranges the folder's music in the order which has been listed on the chalk board by the director. With small slips of cardboard or paper clips he indicates specified hymns and responses—and is completely ready for the enjoyable and profitable rehearsal to come.

When work on one selection is over, the director says, "Next," the accompanist strikes the opening chord(s), and away goes the group on some more of what they came to do in the first place.

"My, how the time has flown!" "It *can't* be that late!" What a sense of pride of accomplishment and satisfaction is the payment where much is accomplished in a short time! Whether your director has an hour and a half or two hours, with intermission, he always finds the time just a little less than he would like to have!

* * * * *

A newly inaugurated music department often encounters a physical plant situation which requires special measures. The committeemen and director may have to survey the available accommodations and come up with workable quarters for your groups.

Below is the copy of the recommendations made by the writer in setting up the music quarters at one church.

Proposed Music Quarters for _____ Church

After careful and detailed study of available rooms in the plans for the new educational building and the present church building, the recommendation is submitted to the church for consideration as quarters for the music department of the church.

Factors determining selection include:

A. Sizes of choirs—thirty-six to forty-eight voices

Your Music Room

B. Use of movable wood risers for providing graduated levels for singers
C. Use of movable sorting racks for quick access to individually assigned music folders (considerable saving in rehearsal time)
D. Space for music filing cabinets, bound book music collections, hymnal cabinets, piano and bench, and conductor's platform
E. Arrangement of chalk boards and bulletin board
F. Robe closets for at least four choirs
G. Office—music
H. Easy access to chancel by choirs
I. Heating and air-conditioning; separate operating from remainder of building
J. Non-interference from, or with other church activities

Recommendations

It is recommended that:
1. The basement room under the chancel of the church be remodeled for the use of the choirs and music groups. The remodeling is to include:
   A. Tile flooring
   B. Fluorescent lighting
   C. Installation of air-conditioning
   D. Possible additional acoustical material on walls similar to present ceiling
   E. Cutting door in east end of room to permit egress to robe room through boiler room
   F. Installation of electric outlets for recording and other equipment
2. That the present robe room be continued in its capacity with the installation of ten feet of additional space for closets on the east side of the room
   A. To provide sufficient space for robes of all choirs
3. That upon the establishment of the pastor's office in the new building, the present office west of the chancel be utilized for music office

A. Music office can be used, and music room can be used simultaneously

Equipment Needed

MUSIC ROOM

1. Piano, studio console type with bench— one each
2. Adult chairs, steel folding, posture— forty each
3. Children's chair, steel folding, posture— forty each
4. Music sorting racks, wheeled, 2′x7′— two each*
5. Filing cabinets, steel, four drawer, 54″x26″x15″— twelve each
6. Cupboard for bound anthem books (now in robe room)— one each
7. Hymnal cabinet, individual compartmented, two shelves 5′x5½′x20″— one each
8. Cupboard for organ music, now in robe room— one each
9. Sectional riser, plywood, movable, 5′x4′x6¾″— twelve each*
10. Chalk boards: 4′x16′— one each
    4′ x 6′— two each
11. Bulletin board, 4′x8′— one each
12. Fixtures for hanging charts on wall—
13. Music stands, metal, adjustable— thirty-six each
14. Director's platform (podium) 3′x3′x8″— one each*
15. Director's stand, with extra shelf— one each
16. Coat and hat racks—
17. Dolly, or glider for piano— one each

ROBE ROOM

1. Additional closet for robes 2½′x10′— one each
2. Mirror— one each
3. Small table— one each

MUSIC OFFICE

1. Desk, executive type— one each
2. Chair, office— one each
3. Typewriter table— one each
4. Bookcase or shelving—

* Can be made locally.

5. Open shelving—
6. Chair, guest— two each
7. Filing cabinet, steel, four-drawer, legal,
   or cap size, with lock— one each

Why list all of these details? Well, it sometimes helps to know what it takes to get a program going, with the minimum "working tools" for the installation. It may help to convince your board, if they need convincing, for them to know what other music departments are working with or consider to be the absolute essentials to begin a program! When your needs are presented in a business-like fashion, with good common-sense reasons to back them up, your battle is practically won!

CHAPTER 18

EQUIPMENT

The heart of every music room is a piano of first quality. A small grand is the most desirable if space and money permit. If an upright must be resorted to, it should be of studio size, not the smaller spinet type. When your director recommends an excellent grade of a standard make, support him fully in this investment. Only the best made instrument can withstand the hard and constant use in a music room and produce the quality of sound needed for your choirs.

Your adult chairs should be of the folding type, which will hold singers in an upright, good posture for singing. Again, consult your director. If your younger choirs are using this room, an investment in a similar set of junior size folding chairs will be needed.

The music stands mentioned earlier for director and singers should be of the solid desk type which will furnish unbroken backing for anthem copies when singers wish to make penciled notes during rehearsals.

A tape recorder upon which the choir can hear itself from time to time is one of the most convincing and valuable training

Equipment

aids your music director can employ. He will be glad to show you its many uses. Again, choose the type with the wide range of frequency pickup and the higher speed of recording over the cheaper but inadequate machines designed for speech only.

A stop watch such as the athletic departments use is invaluable for timing anthems, responses, and other portions of the service.

A metronome is a "must." Nearly every selection has indicated upon it the approximate speed at which the number should be sung and played. The metronome is a device which can be set to indicate any practical recurrence of beats for musicians.

With one of his larger choirs the author used the following arrangement of chalk boards to good advantage. Selections to be rehearsed were listed on both upright boards. Everyone in the room could thus see easily and instantly. The center board was used for brief announcements and working out rhythm and pitch problems as they would occur during the period. (See page 144.)

The large sorting rack was mentioned in the Music Room chapter because it is an essential part in the room itself. This kind of rack is available from several school equipment manufacturers, or it may be made by a carpenter in the church. In one church served by the writer, a local funeral home furnished a beautiful set of rubber-tired wheels for the purpose! The back of this rack was ideal for our bound copies of anthems and collections, and for our hymnals until the hymnal rack by the door could be built. Our choir took particular pride in its rack put together and stained by husbands of two of the members.

One thing to think about, however: our choir family which was in charge of assembling this rack put it together in their basement. When it was finished, beautifully stained and rubbed, they discovered—yes, you guessed it! It was too large to be removed via any opening available! There was nothing to do but take it apart carefully, re-assemble it outside, and move it to its final destination!

In chapter 17 we listed as an example the principal items needed to put our program into action. The following pages contain an announcement which was later distributed to every church member and attendant. This announcement included a revised list of needed items, the unit cost, and the total cost. The purpose? First, to enable all those who had declared, "I can't sing, but I'll be glad to help in some other way!" a chance to make good on their word. Second, to inform every member just what a music program costs, and what is involved.

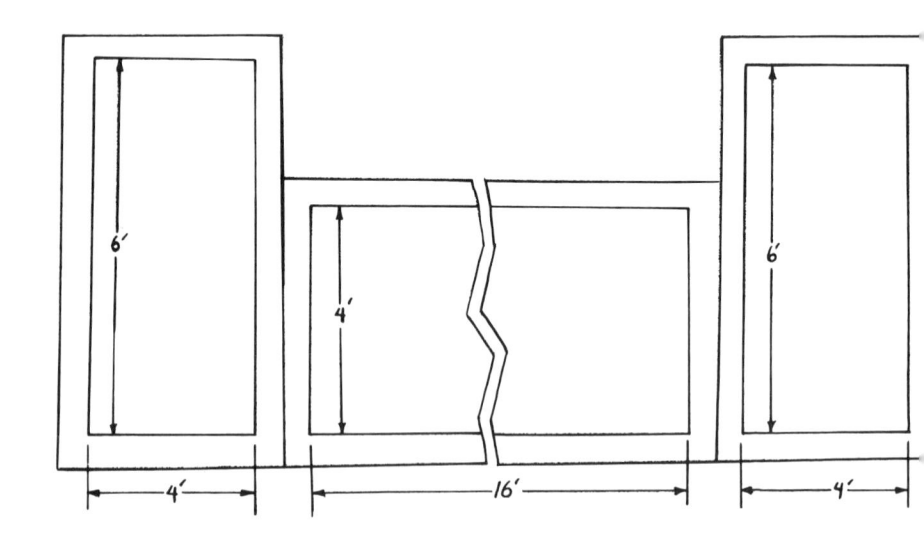

The subsequent combined individual contributions, substantial and modest, constituted a tremendous boost toward our goal.

Equipment 145

The giver with limited means had the pride of knowing he had contributed a music stand or two children's chairs.

To Our Congregation

MUSIC DEPARTMENT EQUIPMENT AND FACILITIES

This list represents those items which will make it possible for our choirs and other music groups of the church to function to the fullest of their capacities. It is not expected that all the furnishings will be provided the first month, or even possibly during the first year. However, this is the goal of our actual needs.

We, ourselves, are going to work to provide some of them. Others will be given by people and organizations wishing to render their church a genuine and lasting service. Our budget is going to be taxed to its utmost in the furnishing of such necessities as music and robes for our expanding choirs. Therefore this equipment which can do so much to make a good choir into a superb one in each division must in the main be provided by us and interested friends.

One big step has already been taken. The gift of the new tile floor in the music room is already there for us to see and enjoy! With this big boost in the right direction it should not be long before the other needed improvements and items begin to make their appearance. God surely richly blesses him who gives of his substance in such a worthy cause!

I am sure you will give this matter your prayers, your thoughts, your efforts. As we remember our music department slogan: *"To our Lord—only our best!"* we can be sure our results will be right!

Minister of Music

(A third sheet of requirements)

MUSIC ROOM RENOVATION AND IMPROVEMENT

Paint for redecorating walls and ceiling

Lighting: Minimum of power of fifty-foot candles at chair height throughout room for sustained reading of music. Arrange two-way switches either entrance of room. Librarians can work at east end of room without burning all room lights. Lights controlled from either end of room. Outlets for lights over bulletin boards. Power and light outlets in each side and each end of room. Lights in robe rooms. Provide outside stairway light (west) with outdoor switch at top of stairs.

Curtains

Muffling organ motor cabinet door without shutting off supply of air required for bellows.

Cutting opening (door) in east wall and placing inset for cabinets.

Building choir robe cabinets along east entrance to room.

EXPANSION OF ROBE ROOM FACILITIES

Additional robe closet 2'6"x11' constructed along east wall.

Interior lock to be installed on door leading to chancel to permit locking of robes, since church is kept unlocked.

Two mirrors, 2'x3' minimum.

One vanity table.

One chair.

The Organ

The purchase of an organ for the sanctuary is an individual problem for each church. Much careful consultation and planning should precede such a step. For this, the committee must lean heavily on its music leader for counsel, and should enlist the opinions of recognized music leaders within an available area. Ascertain what your local electronic organ dealers can offer, by all means. Be just as painstaking, however, to determine what excellent pipe organs can be purchased with the money you can make available.

Many of the good electronic organs today will serve for small chapels. For medium and larger sanctuaries, however, and for any growing church, the music committee should carefully investigate pipe organs which could fill its current and future needs.

See "American Guild of Organists" reference in Appendix.

The writer will not state that the electronic organ can never sound as good as a pipe organ! To this date, however, no electronic instrument can successfully compete with its pipe counterpart! Added amplifiers, multiple sound gadgets, and amazing varieties of the basic electronic "squeal" are offered to the buyer, but organ authorities still hold that the original beauty of the genuine pipe organ tone has not yet been matched! This fact can be verified easily by anyone who wishes to survey a valid cross section of churches of all sizes, organists, and organ teachers of this country.

Music committee members can help tremendously in finding out the item costs and other facts of procurement. Just think how much you can help, too, in reaching congregation members to add their help. Many of you know some individuals well enough to give them that little extra nudge toward doing something worthwhile for the cause! You can help your director in making up budget items for both basic equipment and for upkeep. Relieving him of these time-consuming necessities will be most appreciated!

CHAPTER 19

YOUR MUSIC LIBRARY

The sheet music, anthem collections, and hymn books constitute the chief tools with which your choirs will be working. Like other first-rate tools, these assets need constant and detailed care if their users are to employ them effectively.

The first requirement is adequate protection and storage of the individual numbers. Either the steel filing cabinet or the cardboard shelf box is adequate if properly used. After years with both kinds of library the writer prefers the filing cabinet as being the most flexible for a growing library (both in number of selections and in adding copies for new members). Your music director should make the choice—he has to live with it, supervise it, and make it work.

The word "supervise" is repeated to emphasize the fact that all of the actual receiving, marking, measure numbering, mending, and issuing and collecting of music should be done by persons especially appointed to the job—*not* the director. A minimum of two people will be needed as librarians for each choir, at least for the intermediate through the adult groups. For the older choirs both librarians will be busy at times. The chief reason is, however, that at least *one* such person may be prepared and present for *every* rehearsal and appearance of the choir.

In some choirs the librarian also assists with checking the attendance. While it is highly desirable that the librarian be somewhat familiar with music, some of the most faithful and efficient helpers I have had have been recruited from people who declared, "I can't carry a tune anyway, but I'd like to help!"

When the chorister comes in on Thursday night and takes from the sorting rack his folder containing the selections designated for the evening, someone has had to do many things to make sure his music would be ready. Using the director's list (funished to him far enough ahead of time) the librarian selects the required jackets of anthems and goes to the sorting rack where he has spread out the individual folders. By placing one copy of the anthem on the outside of each folder he knows every singer is supplied. When this process has been repeated with each anthem, all copies are placed inside the folder.

When the rack is used for one choir the folders remain spread out for the next service or meeting. Where several groups must use the same rack, the librarian must gather and distribute the folders for each organization.

Immediately after each service the anthem(s) just used is/are removed from the folders. Before being returned to the jacket, copies are checked for worn-through joints or tears, and mended. Thus, each anthem is always ready for the next use.

The new numbers for study are distributed in the folders, and all is in readiness for the next evening's work.

This kind of organized rehearsal procedure, universally accepted by trained directors, is outlined here in order that the committee members may appreciate the key importance of the assistants in this area.

As each new anthem is received, copies should be numbered consecutively and stamped with the church's name. This provides accurate checking when members may wish to sign parts out for home practice. More and more, directors are having the measures numbered (every five measures) for quick reference in practice—another excellent timesaver, and worth many times the time it takes.

Your director will doubtless wish to have a three-way card index inventory of selections:
1. By name of selection
2. By composer
3. By category (general, Christmas, Easter, etc.)

Suitable 3"x5" cards listing all information are available from nearly every church music publishing company.

Over a period of time, the investment in music can become a considerable one. Is it not just plain common sense to take good care of it? When your choir has but one evening's rehearsal per week is it not wise to encourage the best use of those hours available?

CHAPTER 20

YOUR INSTRUMENTAL PROGRAM

At a time when more young people are learning to play musical instruments than ever before in the history of our country, too many of us are overlooking the potential for band, orchestra, and small ensemble music in our church life! We are failing to realize that this is one more means by which live, active youth may be attracted to, and held within the church's influence.

The author has earlier mentioned his policy of accepting to choir membership otherwise qualified individuals who were not at first professed Christians. So many of them came to the choir because they loved to sing and after a period of association with us decided to make Christ their Savior, too. The instrumental groups also serve to reach young people who otherwise might be lost to the church.

An orchestra brightens the church school assembly period. Many of the social functions are enhanced by this group. Incidental music for dinners and receptions is always in demand.

Greater emphasis upon quartets, trios, and other small ensembles will not only help to have them present for church meetings—it will encourage them to play together in the home. Should we not be stimulating our young people to be praising their Maker through their instruments as well as their voices?

The majesty and dignity of the brass choir lend an unforgettable intensity to the color of the Easter service. The complete orchestra provides the adequate backdrop for the annual oratorio. The band enlivens the annual picnics and fairs. Once the church becomes aware of them, there will be few seasons when your instrumental groups will not be in considerable demand.

One committee member assigned to the instrumental program will be a busy one! If the risers have been made large enough for players as well as singers (see chapter 17) and music stands have been purchased, two of the problems are solved already.

The acquisition of general, sacred, and secular music, accompaniments to hymns and other fellowship songs, and numbers for particular occasions will be most useful. Library organization comparable to that of the choirs will be involved.

With a real going program the church will want to investigate the practicability of purchasing a few of the less commonly owned instruments like the bass viol, the larger horns, and larger percussion instruments.

The young players are there in your community available and eager to play—with good leadership—if you really go after them. What is *your* church doing about them?

CHAPTER 21

ETHICS—PERSONAL RELATIONSHIPS

It would seem that the field of spiritual leadership would be the last place in which problems of personal relationships might occur. However, long experience and observation prove that human frailties sometimes add less-than-beautiful colors to the total picture.

Since successful communication and sympathetic understanding between any members of the church administration and the music staff affect the music program itself and ultimately the entire congregation, these relationships require constant attention and study.

Close and mutual understanding and respect comprise the first requisite. The pastor has the full and final responsibility for the entire church program. The director must recognize that the music is but one part (albeit a vital one) of this program, and that his dreams and desires for effective implementation must be fitted into the overall plans and capabilities of the church. Full study and comprehension of the church's complete operation will better enable him to fulfill his ministry in music.

On the other hand the pastor should take full advantage of the specialized knowledge and skills of his music staff members, respecting and utilizing the professional suggestions from those who have concentrated in their particular field. He naturally holds his music director responsible for success, and for coordinating the activities of the organist and other members of the music staff. Constant and continuing *two-way* liaison between the minister and his director is the only means by which the music of the church can be effective.

Members of the music committee must know the potential of the church, the policies which have been established, and the best ways by which these policies may be implemented. What better way can they accomplish this than by active participation in at least one of these areas as outlined in this text?

As a first step in establishing future relationship the pastor and his music committee, music member of the church board, superintendent of education and/or other personnel responsible for this area should sit down and determine exactly what their church needs in the way of music leadership. The music director, if they have one, should participate too, of course. If they are not sure just what their needs are, or from what point their program should start, they can obtain help from a number of sources.

Churches with balanced programs in operation, trained church directors and ministers of music, college church music instructors, modern practical church music texts in our public and college libraries—all can make helpful contributions from which planners can choose for their particular situation.

Once their program is decided upon the obvious next step is defining exactly the areas of duties of the director. Where no director is yet hired, these areas are discussed with candidates for the position. They determine together—*before employment*—just how much will be expected for the money and time available. Easily ninety percent of the friction which sometimes develops can be laid to a lack of this preliminary agreement between parties.

"Oh, but," you say, "this could never happen to *us!* We have always gotten along wonderfully in our church!" Let me cite a few of the many cases when this did happen.

Shortly after arriving in El Paso the writer was visited by a minister, also a newcomer, from another church. "I have a problem the like of which I have never before encountered," he began. "One morning during my first week in the office a young man walked in, reached over to shake my hand, and said, 'I am _____ _____, your director of music. You take care of your preaching; I'll take care of the music; and we'll get along just fine!'

"Had you been in my place what would you have done?" he asked. My answer was immediate and emphatic. "That young man would have remained in the employ of the church just long enough for me to say two words: 'You're fired!' "

In an extreme case like this where the individual was completely lacking in concept of both his job and common courtesy only extreme remedial actions could be the answer.

How did this all come about? The young director obviously had had no training for his job as a leader of worship music. The earlier minister had evidently accepted him without defining obligations or in any way establishing an agreement on relationships.

Why, it is difficult to understand, but breaches of common decency and business procedures occur too often in the matter of terminating relationships. A period of a least one month is normally the shortest notice which should be given by either employer or employee.

One director in a local church announced three weeks before Christmas that he was leaving immediately to take a position in another city. With not one word of warning and in the middle of this critical time of preparation of the Christmas music he took off.

Several questions immediately come to mind. What were his inner thoughts relative to the groups he had left in a time of need? Whom could he expect to give him a recommendation at some future date? How could the church to which he went know that he would not in turn desert them in like manner?

Music directors by no means have a monopoly on the sins in this field. Not too long ago a choir director was approached by a friend. "I understand that _____ _____ has been hired to take over your job. I didn't know you were leaving!" Stunned, the woman could only reply weakly, "I didn't know either!"

Having received no intimation that any dissatisfaction with her work existed, or that any change was contemplated, the woman went straight to the minister. He denied all knowledge of any such action. The director then called the other leader in question and learned that in truth she had on an earlier date definitely been offered the position.

Together the director and her husband confronted the minister. He finally admitted his guilt in the matter!

Does a person who stoops to such underhanded practices deserve *any* position of authority, of all places a minister of the Gospel? What kind of spiritual leader could such a person profess to be?

I wish that such instances were only the figments of bad dreams, but unfortunately they are true much too often in our manmade houses of God in this world of ours! If the writer appears to have been hammering repeatedly on this subject in this book, it is simply in the hope that its readers may be stirred to action to establish and maintain honest and business-like relationships.

Pastors with current music programs, part- or full-time, can and should insure against much potential future trouble by putting down in writing, right now (see chapters 4 and 6), with their music leaders, the established policies and procedures for future reference and use. While the present situation may be rosy with spoken or tacit agreement on all major points, an unexpected change in either department can produce chaos.

The director who consistently shares in the planning and determining of policies with which he is directly concerned, and who is thoroughly cognizant of the close interrelationship between his work and that of every other department will be a much more valuable person to the entire church. If he is unable or unwilling to share in such planning, then the church can be expected to look for a person who will want to do so.

Ethics, Personal Relationships

The minister must not be disappointed at a lack of interest and enthusiasm if he shuts out his staff in such planning. He must demonstrate that he is big enough to be a true leader by seeking and accepting counsel of his specialized assistants. In like manner the specialist must be ready to see some of his ideas modified or adapted to fit a balanced program.

The music committee? You can do much to act as a balance wheel. When differences of opinion occur, as they most assuredly will, courageously sitting down together and frankly discussing the difficulties will lead to an acceptable solution in a surprising number of instances.

And the Lord has a way of being most helpful when called upon for guidance in such matters!

CHAPTER 22

IMPROVING MUSIC FACILITIES

A director often inherits a situation which is considerably less than desirable, both from the standpoint of getting the job done at all, and from the existence of small(?) conveniences which build a group spirit in the whole department. While conditions in the following were similar to those described in an earlier chapter, they are outlined below because of several different factors involved, and because the total program contemplated was somewhat smaller.

The following survey was presented to the music committee and later to the board of a certain church. No one of them had realized fully the difficulties under which the department had been trying to function, and no one on the music staff had bothered to tell them anything about what should be done. (How often are we guilty of complaining, "Why don't they _____ _____?" to ourselves or to friends, instead of going in a straightforward manner to the people who *could* do something about it?) We music people must take the blame for not educating our congregations as to working needs of the program.

Action was taken on the recommendations made, and we were at once provided with somewhat improved accommodations until much better room arrangements could be approved and completed. The survey may serve as a suggestion to any of you who may need to have your present conditions revised. Take the trouble and time to advise them *why* present ways are detrimental, and *why* and *how* changes must be made.

It will be noted that the music table was advised and accepted until our sorting rack could be made. The anthems were placed in individual stacks. As each singer arrived he picked up one of each and placed all in his folder.

Music Program Requirements

(Survey of needs presented upon occasion of accepting a new position)

Main Music Hall: 24'x30' minimum
  Essential: fifty chairs, folding or writing arm type
          one piano
          one director's podium
          one table 10'x1½'
          one blackboard 3'x10' minimum
          forty junior chairs
          one bulletin board
  Availability: First priority for music groups
  Location: 1. Where music activities can be conducted without interference with, or from other groups
           2. Easily accessible to main church
  Acoustics: Treatment with whatever amount of acoustical material needed to achieve proper sound conditions
  Lighting: Adequate to produce forty- to fifty-foot candles of power for reading
  Ventilation: Sufficient for groups of fifty
Highly Desirable
  Risers: In progressive 6" levels, portable or permanent floor construction
  Heating system: Separate, with cut-off valves

>Access from outside without having to go through rest of church
>Buzzer system connected to pastor's study

Advantages:
>This hall is multi-purpose. It would be available and entirely suitable for other church meetings and functions when not needed for music groups. Where this type room has been installed it has developed to be the most in demand for other meetings, too.
>
>This room is suitable for vocal and instrumental needs contemplated in the long-range program for the church, as well as for current use. Robe rooms and library can be securely shut off from main hall, and locked.

Library: Spaces to be provided for:
>Twelve standard letter size 4-drawer file cabinets
>One desk
>One table 2½'x5' minimum (sorting, mending, stamping music)
>Four more files will be needed for music now crowded into wall cupboard
>Door equipped with lock

Robe Rooms: At least two rooms, each 10'x14' minimum
>Essential: One for men's robes and wraps
>One for women's robes and wraps
>Junior choir robes may be divided between adult rooms for the present
>Wardrobes, senior, built-in, with sliding doors
>Wardrobes, junior height, equipped as above
>Mirror, one full-length for each robe room
>Doors equipped with locks

Alternate plan: Three robe rooms:
>One for men; one for women; one for junior choir
>Powder, or bathroom facilities highly desirable for women's robe room

The quarters described constitute the minimum needs for the music department of _____ Church.

Music Quarters — Proposed

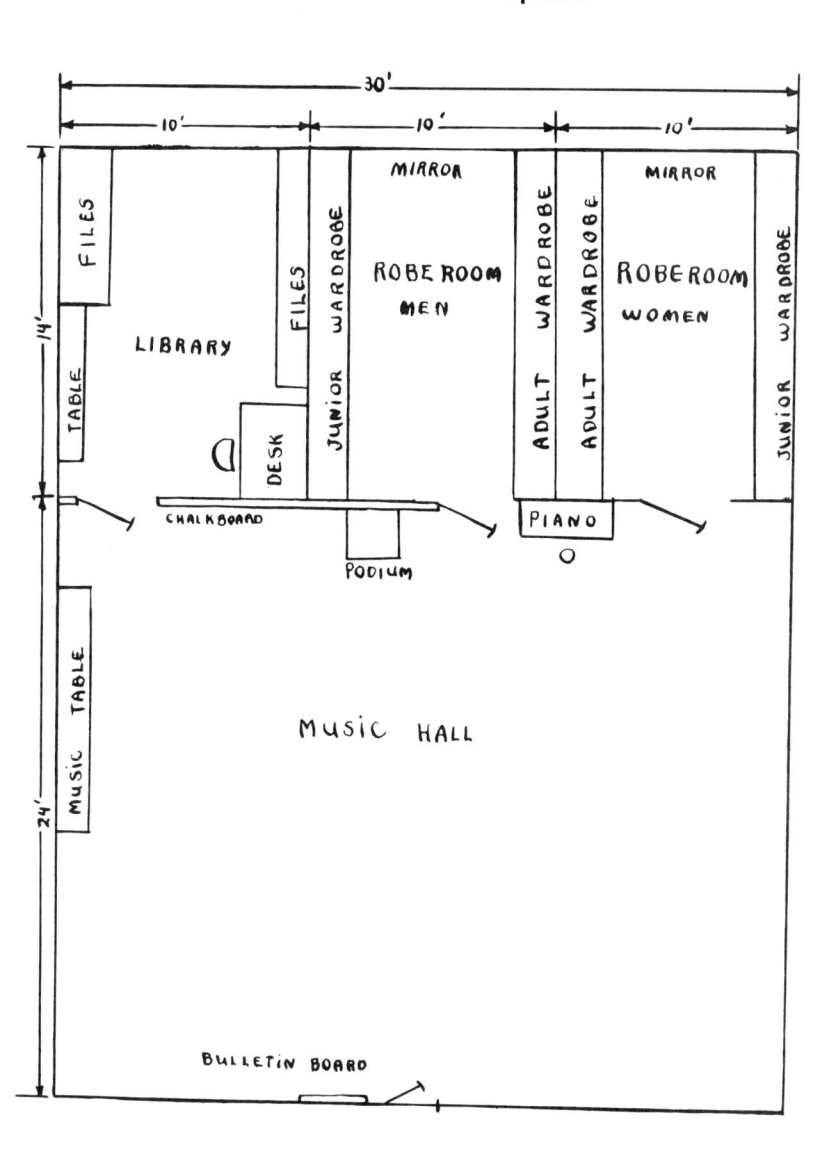

The music hall of these dimensions permits maximum use of space and will serve all music groups as well as being available to other church meetings when not needed by the singers.

The library should adjoin the music hall to eliminate unnecessary carrying of music.

Locks on music and robe rooms permit required securing of property when music hall is used for other groups.

Blackboard on front wall is needed for all music ensembles and music reading classes.

Group members obtain copies of music to be sung from table at side of room at beginning of meeting, and return music at end of period. No time is wasted passing out and collecting numbers during practice.

Present arrangement is unsatisfactory and wasteful of time and energy.

Rehearsals with piano are required. In preliminary work organ is unsuitable, as it covers up many mistakes. Organ should be used for final preparation only, after choir is sure of its parts.

The small chapel, which is the only room where lighting approaches adequacy, thanks to the interest and action of your pastor and custodian, is at great distance from the so-called library.

At least twenty minutes before each rehearsal is required to carry books, music, and material to the room. Blackboard must be found and carried to room. After practice the same amount of time is required to reverse the process and leave room in condition for other use.

When the chapel is needed for another group, the choir is shunted to the primary room in basement where the lighting is poor. When dining room, too, is in use, choir is ousted from the primary room!

In short, the body of men and women you expect to furnish a major part of your public Sunday worship is presently surviving in a most precarious manner, and unable to do the quality of work they would prefer to do for you all!

The current situation is far from being conducive to encour-

Improving Music Facilities

aging volunteer choir members to continue attendance. Time and energy now consumed in "stevedore" work before and after each practice could be used much more profitably on the music itself and with individual conferences and individual training and help.

The so-called music library is totally inadequate from the standpoint of space and availability. In addition it is overrun by other activities and objects. Flower vases, urns, stands, altar candelabra, candles, and other articles foreign to a music library occupy so much of the space in the present room that proper functioning of the library is impossible. With the library placed next to the music hall the present room off the chancel could be used fully for the articles listed above!

Many hours of plain hard work will be needed to put the present music in order. Copies of anthems out of place, torn pages, and worn-out jackets indicate that for many years the practice has been to use music for Sunday, then just drop it anywhere without returning it to anything like its alphabetical file. Your director should better spend his time on this project, along with what librarian help he can muster, than on transporting the materials to and from whatever room *happens* to be available to the choir on rehearsal night.

It is strongly recommended that immediate action be taken by the council to provide the facilities herein outlined, beginning with those marked essential, to enable your men and women to begin doing the kind of work of which they are so capable.

Director of Music

* * * * *

You music committeemen can help your director tremendously in keeping your congregation and key committees advised as to what is required by your singing groups.

If your author seems to be repeating some similar items in several of these outlines, he is doing so in order to assist the non-musical helpers as they draw up pertinent information for the director.

CHAPTER 23

THE CHOIR REHEARSAL

"What do you all do down there for a whole evening, when your choir selection takes up only about five minutes in the service?" Just about every director and many of your choristers have been the target of this, and similar questions at one time or another. Husbands and wives of singers often fail to understand the need of an entire evening's work.

To answer just such questions our adult choir staged a "How We Do It" program following a church supper one night. When the dishes were cleared away everyone sat around the tables enjoying several of our best-loved hymns.

Then I said, "Let's turn to number 124." Our accompanist played the introduction and started what turned out to be almost a piano solo! About halfway through I stopped them. "What's the trouble?" I asked our crowd.

"Oh, we don't know this one," came the replies.

"All right, let's learn it! This is a beautiful one," I suggested.

Meanwhile, members of the choir had quietly withdrawn to obtain their folders and assemble on the risers behind the cur-

The Choir Rehearsal

tains at the end of the end of the dining room. The congregation had thus not had the support of the music readers in the new number.

I then proceeded to teach them the new hymn. First, all of us read the words of stanza one aloud. Then through the cumulative phrase rote method we learned pitch and duration of the notes and words. Finally we returned to concentrate our attention on the meaning and significance of the hymn's message.

I glanced at my watch. "That was twenty-one minutes well-spent, wasn't it? You have now made the acquaintance of a grand, new hymn!"

It was then pointed out that as leaders of the music in the service their choirs had to learn all hymns, responses, and anthems well enough to portray the full spiritual message after learning the right notes and correct parts. By now our crowd could understand from firsthand experience something of what our singers had to go through.

The curtains were now pulled back, revealing our choir in position. We then proceeded through a typical rehearsal, cutting each part of the period into segments just long enough to show our listeners what was happening. Our spokesman explained each step as we proceeded.

The large chart of the night's work (on p. 166) showed clearly how our period was planned. The need and similarity of our vocal warm-up exercises to those of the athlete was brought out. First attention to final polish for hymns, responses, and the anthem for Sunday was to be expected.

"Woodshedding," working out more difficult spots in the music for the following Sunday, was next order of business. Technically, the notes and parts of this music would be well under control permitting more emphasis on meaning now.

The slightly familiar music came in for another reading, and brief, but pithy corrections in places of wrong notes or faulty parts. The "sight-reading" (actually recognition of old friend rhythm patterns and familiar skips in new combinations) presented new numbers to be used three weeks hence.

1. Warmup
2. Hymns: 12, 117, 86
3. Response: 418
4. With a Voice
5. Psalm of Thanksgiving } Sunday
6. Greater Love Hath -
    Measures 24-32, 54-60
7. Psalm 150
    From change of key to end.
    [Intermission]
8. Hymn 136
9. O Savior Blest - Attn. to descant
10. Glorious, Everlasting
11. Surely the Lord
12. Come Down, Lord } Sight Read
13. Upstairs w/ organ

The Choir Rehearsal

In a regular rehearsal the final work of the evening consists of going through Sunday's anthem in the choir loft with the organ. Here, any minor changes in organ registration can be made and adjustments of balance of voice parts finalized. While we did not move everyone to the sanctuary for it this night, our listeners could see why we did it.

"Why not just work on Sunday's numbers for the whole evening?" was asked. "How much of all the stuff we sat up late cramming for that examination back in school do we remember?" I inquired in reply. Smiles all around. Hammering time after time on the same number is not only deadly, but even disastrous to interest. It is one of the best ways to lose choristers and alienate people!

The variety of study and of problems keeps interest pitch at a high level through the evening. Psychologically, the four separate shorter periods of study for each selection make the learning deeper and comprehension more thorough.

An additional advantage of this kind of rehearsal lies in the fact that when a business man just has to be out of town one week, or a housewife has a head cold one night, the three remaining weeks of acquaintance with the music make it possible for these people still to do an acceptable job with their associates. Under proper guidance this arrangement does *not* constitute encouragement or condoning of spotty or occasional attendance.

On another chart (p. 168) we traced the music sight-read: (1) through slightly familiar (2) nearly ready (3) and immediate, or ready for Sunday (4) steps to show the planned continuity.

Needless to say, this was one of the best evenings we had ever invested in terms of congregation understanding and appreciation.

Not every director will use exactly the same order. The effective leader does plan and utilize carefully the time and talent at hand, however.

Perhaps via this chapter more of our laymen and clergy can better understand the need for advanced planning between music director and minister. Your choirs—dedicated volunteers, most

ALLOCATION OF REHEARSAL TIME

Music—First Week	Music—Second Week	Music—Third Week	Music—Fourth Week
Warm-up Exercises	Warm-up	Warm-up	Warm-up
Immediate Music for Sunday { Hymns, Anthems, Responses }	Immediate	Immediate	(4) Immediate
Nearly Ready	Nearly Ready	(3) Nearly Ready	Nearly Ready
Slightly Familiar	(2) Slightly Familiar	Slightly Familiar	Slightly Familiar
(1) Sight Reading (New Music)	Sight Reading	Sight Reading	Sight Reading
Immediate Review of music for Sunday with organ	Immediate	Immediate	Immediate

The Choir Rehearsal

of them—will sing their hearts out to do for the service what you want done—if you will help them to prepare it.

Don't hamstring them by announcing to your director on Friday night or Sunday morning, "By the way, I'm preaching on topic 'X' instead of subject 'Y' as I had planned, so we'd like the choir to sing _____!" This is not only "dirty pool," it is the act of a so-called leader who knows much less about his job than he should.

To the rare but genuine emergency which can happen to any of us they will respond with the same loyalty and dedication they give you the rest of the year—when you show them you understand and appreciate what they are doing.

CHAPTER 24

BUDGETING

Like any other part of the church program the music department costs money. The expense of salaries, materials, and other factors must be carefully planned and executed if the department is to succeed.

Under the guidance of your music director the outline of the actual needs for the year will be set up. When these plans have been approved by the church governing body, it will be the job of you in the music committee to help the director administer the budget.

It is only businesslike to place the music program on the same definite level as the set amount allowed for the pastor's salary, the mortgage payments, and the utilities. Most churches prefer to determine a certain percentage of the total budget for its music activities. How do you arrive at this percentage? Simply set up the cost, for a year, of the total of the items which all of you have decided upon. What percentage of the total church budget does this consist?

Should there be any question about what percent your size church should be using in this respect, your committee can easily secure information from other churches of approximately your size that have thriving programs in music.

Aside from the salaries, the remainder of the budget will ordinarily be set up under two or more headings:

Capital Outlay: Those items which will be needed for more or less permanent equipment for the church. Such items as:

| pianos | filing cabinets | new hymnals |
| robes | reference library | music stands |

Maintenance: Items which wear out comparatively quickly; repairs and maintenance of present equipment:

music	robes: mending and cleaning
music mending and repairs	church school materials
rebinding hymnals, anthem collections	office supplies
	postage
piano and organ tuning and repair	

When the whole budget has been approved it would be helpful to set up an informal accounting system like the following, with a separate item for each of the individual headings (with the amounts allotted to each):

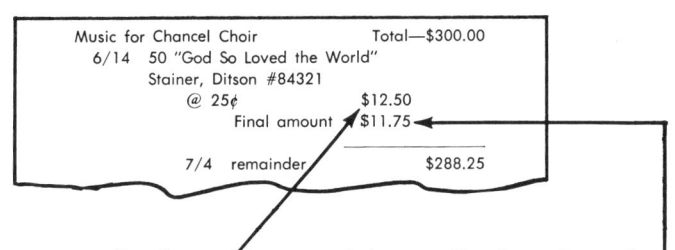

```
    Music for Chancel Choir          Total—$300.00
    6/14  50 "God So Loved the World"
          Stainer, Ditson #84321
              @ 25¢                    $12.50
                     Final amount      $11.75

          7/4  remainder                $288.25
```

This amount, listed cost, is entered *in pencil,* when the order is placed. When the music is received and the amount billed, the discount (if any) is deducted, the postage is added and the final total is entered in ink.

With this simple system it is always possible to tell at a glance how much money has been spent, what amount obligated, and what is left in each section of the total fund.

CHAPTER 25

PLANNING FOR THE FUTURE

In the early months of your music program, and later on, every year or so, you will doubtless wish to conduct a congregation-wide survey for several purposes:
1. To inform your people of what is going on in the department. (It is amazing how little some people are aware of the activities of the church if they are not directly involved.)
2. To apprise them of opportunities for participation and training.
3. To let them know about the needs of your growing program. (The Lord nudges many to help when the need is placed squarely before them.)

The survey below is similar to other outlines in other chapters, but it does contain features not presented before. Incidentally, the writer has never initiated a survey like this, to the accompaniment of some deep and sincere prayers, that did not result in some happy outcomes!

As a result of this one we gained:
    a. Several members for both choirs
    b. Money for the first movable sorting racks—and a beautiful set of wheels from a mortuary firm!

Planning for the Future

    c. Money for four additional robes
    d. Enough filing material to set up our library
    e. Many helpful and constructive suggestions and offers to help

Most important of all, we brought the people to the realization that this was *their* program, that this was a part of their worship that directly concerned *them*.

MUSIC_RESOURCES_SURVEY
_____ Church

WE NEED YOUR OPINION ! ! !
    WHETHER YOU SING OR NOT,

the planning of your music program for the next three years requires your opinion on a number of important questions. Your suggestions and help on topics and projects included in this outline will be valuable to you and to us. Improvement of music in your worship and church life will depend to a great extent upon your reply. Please see to it that this reply reaches the church office not later than
    SUNDAY, OCTOBER 9th

                                     Thank you,
                                     Lynn W. Thayer

Time required:

Reading time: $5\frac{1}{2}$ minutes
Listing suggestions: You're on your own!
Completing applications: $1\frac{1}{4}$ minutes
                September 30, 19___

Current Music Activities

CHURCH MUSIC PROGRAM

I'm sure you have some pretty definite ideas about music in the regular morning worship, the Sunday school, and in other departments of your church. On the last sheets of this survey you will find opportunity to express yourselves fully. If additional copies are needed for others in your family, a call to the church office will bring them to you without delay.

MUSIC READING CLASS (ADULTS) BEGINNERS

Most of us like to sing. Not all of us had a chance to learn to read music in school, however. There is nothing specially magical, mysterious, or difficult in learning to follow the notes in our songs. What a difference it makes in our enjoyment of music when we can pick up a new hymn or song—and *sing* it—in just the same way we read news items in our newspaper!

You can learn to do this in the Music Reading Class *without* cost, except for the textbook ($1.25). Tuesday evenings at 7:00 o'clock there are others just like you starting in on this fun, too. Why not come along and really enjoy yourself? The class last season included men and women from four other churches who asked to be included in this privilege. Several such inquiries have already been received this Fall.

You have first chance! What will you do with it?

ADVANCED MUSIC READING CLASS

If you have had some experience in reading and would like to review and brush up, this is the place for it. Folks from the beginners' class of last year (some of whom are singing professionally and are here improving their reading technique) are doing more advanced things and enjoying themselves at the same time! This group meets at 8:05 on Tuesday evenings. Again, no cost to you above the textbook.

SONG LEADERS AND ACCOMPANISTS

Our church needs song leaders and accompanists for many of its functions—you, yourself, know how often! You who have a background in either piano or voice are eligible for this group.

Fundamentals of song leading, choice of selections for specific occasions, and techniques of working with groups are studied and put into practice. Pianists learn to improve their techniques of playing with, and for others.

Planning for the Future

You who are eligible should enroll immediately in order not to miss the first instruction. Class meets on Wednesday evenings at 8:05.

CHANCEL CHOIR

Our standards for this organization are high. We believe you will agree that they are justly so for this group which has so great a part in our regular public worship. Acceptance of new members for this choir depends upon the following factors (in addition to proper balance of parts):

1. Reasonable background and training in vocal ensemble work
2. At least moderate ability to read music
3. Regular attendance and faithful participation in rehearsals and services of this group

Applicants not fully qualified for participation at this time may become eligible through additional training in the reading class. Application blank is attached.

CHILDREN'S CHOIR

Several boys and girls on the waiting list last season have been called to fill vacancies of those who have graduated from this choir. This thirty-voice aggregation meets for rehearsal at 6:30 on Thursdays. Nearly one hundred percent attendance at rehearsal and Sunday services last season, plus an active and growing waiting list attest to the enthusiasm and enjoyment of these youngsters.

The children's choir has a part in the morning service once each month and on special holidays and occasions. Requirements for membership include:

1. Minimum age of eight years
2. Regular attendance at rehearsals and services
3. Attention and application
4. General good conduct and behavior

Parents who wish the names of their children to be placed on the waiting list and have voice tests may use the blank enclosed.

Whether you sing or not, you can help in one or more of the following ways:

LIBRARIANS

Librarians are needed for both the chancel and children's choirs. Duties include getting out music for rehearsals, putting it away afterward. Anthems have to be mended. Our library is excellent, but it needs to be surveyed, catalogued and completely rearranged for quick, convenient use. Mending and cataloguing can be done during practice periods, if desired. At least four people are needed here.

EQUIPMENT MANAGER

The entire library is to be relocated in a more convenient place. Portable distribution racks are to be made. Arrangement and labeling of new folders will be required. Arrangement of supplementary platforms and seats for special occasions needs direction. Supervision of these jobs will require at least two people.

Equipment Needed

FILING CABINETS

Four standard size four-drawer filing cabinets, new or used (steel is preferred, but wood is acceptable), are badly needed in addition to those we now have, for proper filing of music. Many of our anthems are now piled tightly in a closet where several folders must be moved out before those in back may be found and used! Can *you* get one of these for the church?

CHILDREN'S CHOIR ROBES

As this survey is being compiled, word has been received that the women's association has just voted to buy two more robes for this choir. This gift is deeply appreciated, as it will allow us to accept two more singers! Each robe costs about $18.50. How would you like to outfit the next child?

DISTRIBUTION RACKS

Lumber and fixtures will cost roughly $45.00.

Planning for the Future

CHOIR FOLDERS

(Permanent, cloth-bound) Music folders in robe-matching colors will enhance the appearance of our choirs in worship and increase music's longevity.

FILING AND MENDING MATERIAL

Filing cards (3x5); filing folders (letter size); gummed labels; index cards (3x5); file cabinet, four-drawer, steel, for 3x5 cards; transparent tape; mending; and hinged tape are needed.

* * * * *

You see, there is *something* each one of you can do to help improve the music in your church! If none of these top-priority projects fires your imagination, let us know. Other projects need attention, too. Most of all is needed the *do-ing* by *you*.

Sacrifice? Busy? Other things to do? Of course! Worthwhile people like yourselves always have full schedules. Did you ever accomplish anything worthwhile without sacrificing something else? No, no one else of us has, either!

Can you think of anything that quite takes the place of that little glow of satisfaction that comes with being a part of a live program which brings satisfaction and inspiration to so many?

The above section of this survey is our part. The rest of it is up to you.

We thank you for this chance to consider with you some of the vital aspects of our church program.

Lynn W. Thayer

MY SUGGESTIONS FOR OUR CHURCH MUSIC PROGRAM

Date_____

Music in the Sunday Worship

The most effective music is that in which everyone takes part. What music in the service do you like best?

What ten hymns do you like best?

What new, or less familiar hymns would you like to have sung?

How can our congregational singing be improved?

What music activities would you like to have added to our program?

What other comments would you like to make which might be helpful in planning and operating the program?

Name _____
Address _____
Tel. _____

Be sure to sign all sheets in order that your opinion may be tabulated.

APPLICATION FOR CHANCEL CHOIR

Date_____

I should like to be considered for membership in the Chancel Choir.

Name_____ Tel._____
Address_____ Voice_____
(sop., alto, tenor, bass)

Training:
Experience:
  Note: Please give complete outline of your training and experience.

APPLICATION FOR CHILDREN'S CHOIR

Date_____

I should like to have my son/daughter _____ aged _____ enrolled in the Children's Choir. I understand new members will be accepted in the order of their applications, and as qualified, as vacancies occur in the organization. I will do my part to see that _____ fulfills the requirements of this group.

Signed _____
(parent)
Address _____
Telephone _____

INDICATION OF INTEREST

Date_____

I should like to
- enroll in the class checked below.
- assist in the capacity indicated.
- help the program by providing the articles checked.

Classes
- Beginning sight reading
- Advanced sight reading
- Song leader and accompanist

Areas of service
- Librarian
- Equipment manager
- Other_____

Equipment needed—I should like to help:
- Children's choir robe
- Filing cabinet
- Distribution rack
- Choir folders
- Filing and mending material
- Other _____

Signed _____
Address _____
Telephone _____

As your program grows, so will your investment and your costs. Here again, each of you in being ready to inform the church body of the increased service being rendered in your particular area can help convince them that the returns in God's service are staying well ahead of the costs.

As the services grow in each area, your music director must place an ever-increasing reliance on each of you on the committee. Just what choirs are to be added, and when, plus other expansions of the program have to be worked out with all of you together.

CHAPTER 26

MAINTAINING YEAR-ROUND INTEREST

Your director has discovered that there are periods during the year when the choir enthusiasm is high. Then there can be lulls, or times when it may be less than easy to keep the interest of the singers at a point where they will be eager to be present each week.

The two highest peaks in the year are, of course, Christmas and Easter, with all the special preparations involved. Little difficulty is ordinarily experienced in sustaining interest and attention during these two seasons.

One might say the choristers should be sufficiently dedicated to be present all the time, regardless of "special" or outstanding events. True enough, but remember we are dealing with human beings, with all their frailties and all the carefully fabricated commercial magnets to draw their attention and energies elsewhere.

While formerly many choirs "closed up shop" during the summer and had to start almost "from scratch" again in September, a fast-growing host of churches now keep their choirs together the year round. Don't we need spiritual help and replenishment during the summer? Besides, what better time for re-charging the choir's batteries, too? The presenting of important events all the year keeps the choirs on their toes. The following example is one to be considered.

One director started the year with an adult choir retreat on the weekend following Labor Day. The retreat was set up at the denominational camp high in the pines of the Sacramento Mountains. Since the families were arriving all through the day on Friday, depending on hours they could leave their work, the afternoon was given over to registering, settling in their rooms, and informal chitchats.

By supper time all families were ready for the big bell which summoned all to the dining room. Baby sitters for the smaller tots and counselors for the older youngsters were prepared with programs for the weekend. After supper tired little ones were tucked in bed and the teenagers began their first activities. Gathering in the big living room of the main lodge before a roaring fire, adult choir members received personally marked copies of the oratorio which was to be sung the following February. Each singer listened and followed his score while the entire production was presented by record.

One lady and her son kept a corn popper busy at the fireplace, filling a huge cardboard container with the fluffy white kernels. The "coke" machine on the wall had been well stocked. From time to time a chorister would refill his paper plate from the box, or go to the wall for a drink, then return to his book and have his neighbor point out the place. No other sound interrupted the intense concentration of the entire group for nearly two hours.

The next day's clinician, Dr. E. A. Thormodsgaard, who arrived during the study, was astonished at the sight. "I just can't believe it!" he exclaimed. "Folks simply don't concentrate like this nowadays!"

Saturday was opened by a sunrise worship service out on the hillside chapel overlooking miles of natural beauty. A series of sessions of intensive voice training and choral techniques filled the day for adults. Hikes, nature studies, and group games sharpened the already voracious appetites of the younger set. Family musical stunts and games finished the day.

For Sunday morning the choir had prepared its own complete

worship service for the beautiful camp chapel, since no other regular groups were occupying camp that weekend. The noon meal officially closed the retreat and signaled the beginning of the homeward trek.

The music committee members and choir properties committee had made all preliminary arrangements with the camp management: numbers of children and adults to count for each meal; placing of families in suitable rooms; setting up study and meeting rooms; arranging for care of younger family members; and dozens of other pertinent incidentals.

Summer choir camps are becoming more and more popular in all sections of the country. The cooperation of the lay members of the church is becoming increasingly important.

In the church described above, dedication of all choirs for the year was held on the following Sunday. From that date until the Christmas music preparation started, all time in addition to that required for the weekly anthems and hymns was devoted to familiarization with the oratorio music.

As soon as Christmas concentration began, the oratorio was shelved until January, when intense practice prepared the group for the February date.

The oratorio over, Easter music then claimed undivided attention. Coincidental with the closing of the school year came Children's Sunday and graduation exercises when all choirs together celebrated the "moving up" of those eligible for the next higher group.

What of the summer "doldrums"—the time to which many directors look forward with some dread? Summer choir schools of several weeks each at the church kept the primary and intermediate choirs interested. A judicious mixture of fun and games was enjoyed along with the special training.

This was the time when much attention was devoted to the choir notebooks: very simple ones for the primary singers, and more elaborate ones for the intermediate group. A study of the meaning of the signs and symbols of the church, basic denominational and general church history, meaning of church architecture, significance of the various sections of the worship service—these and more topics were included.

Imaginative leaders can make this cumulative building of such information via self-made notebooks intensely fascinating to boys and girls of these ages. Dads and mothers invariably become deeply interested in these projects, too, and incidentally learn much about their church that *they* didn't know! (See Appendix for listings of excellent texts in this area.)

Pre-arranged exchange visits to other churches in the vicinity and preparation for several multiple-choir programs, some with neighboring denominations, sparked the interest of the members through the summer.

By vote, the older choirs had chosen to stay together for the summer, with each family being absent for the period of the individual vacation. Since the September choir get-together had been so successful, several summer late-Friday and all-day Saturday retreats were arranged where singers of the older choirs could concentrate on devotions and choir training.

Oh, yes, in between times the adult choir managed to find time to record two full sides of a record of familiar hymns. With such a year's program, there is little opportunity for boredom or loss of interest.

What does a full schedule like this mean to the music committee? Let's put it this way: How can such a program be fulfilled *without* an efficient, enthusiastic music committee helping all the way?

May we remind you one more time? By diligent study the wise music committee comes to know what constitutes a good, sensible church-wide music system for its particular "family." It employs a qualified director and orients him completely in all phases of what is expected. Now comes the hard part: it allows *him* to make the working decisions to get the job done.

It stands staunchly behind him as he prayerfully applies the special training required in this field. It backs him honestly and fully in decisions made and policies followed, helping him to meet the pettiness, the carping, and selfishness which occasionally come to the surface wherever many people congregate.

* * * * *

Activity for activity's sake? Organizations just to show fancy charts full of names?

Nowhere can the maxim, "the letter killeth but the spirit giveth life" be more true than in the church music program. Unless reverence, dedication, and a sense of service permeate every fiber of the structure, the whole becomes a gaudy nothing, a sorry shell of meaningless sound and display.

Let us eternally remember that music is justified in our worship in direct proportion to the extent that it helps to draw and hold man closer to God and church; that it helps to bring him the divine power, strength, and inspiration to live a better life with his fellow men today than he did yesterday.

APPENDIX

This appendix or bibliography contains excerpts from "Church Music Texts and Training References" assembled by the author. Listed here are a few of the outstanding texts in the various fields of church music. For the church which is just beginning its program those books marked with the asterisk (*) in each category might prove to be helpful as first purchases.

The author uses many in this list regularly, either as texts or references in connection with the church music classes at the University of Texas at El Paso, and with the numerous church music workshops he is called on to conduct. The reader will find that, even though a book may be listed under one particular heading, it will often contain much valuable material in one or more of the other phases of church music.

The reader is reminded that new publications on the general subject are appearing steadily today, and that he should take every opportunity to keep up to date in what is happening in this area.

The non-music texts are especially recommended to all personnel who are connected in any way with the church's music program—especially the minister of music! If we are to do a good job must we not know *how* this church of ours got to be where it is today? Can we successfully guide its music destinies if we are ignorant of the forces which have shaped it, and the devastating attacks it has weathered? What *are* the fundamentals of faith which so many of us have blithely taken for granted?

As we exercise the precious privilege of working with the souls of others may we be ever mindful of the corresponding obligation to arm ourselves with the best knowledge and information available!

Appendix

General Church Music

Comprehensive Program of Church Music, Whittlesey (Westminster Press)
Music and Worship in the Church, Lovelace & Rice (Abingdon)
Music in My Bible, Grauman (Pacific Press)
Steps Toward a Singing Church, Kettring (Pacific Press)
Music in Worship, Ashton (United Church)
Catholic Church Music, Hume (Dodd-Mead)
Spanish Cathedral Music in the Golden Age, Stevenson (U. of Calif.)
Church Music Manual (Baptist), Sims (Convention Pr.)
The Training of Church Choirs, Sydnor (Abingdon)
Protestant Church Music in America, Davison (E. C. Schirmer)
Church Music, Illusion and Reality, Davison (Harvard U. Pr.)
Patterns of Protestant Church Music, Stevenson (Duke U. Pr.)
Protestant Church Music in America, Stevenson (Norton)
In Every Corner Sing, Clokey (Morehouse-Graham)
Planning for Church Music, Sydnor (Abingdon)
Church Music in Transition, Hooper (Broadman)
Choir Ideas, Breck (Wilde)
Make His Praise Glorious (Excell)
The Instrumental Ensemble in Church, Trobian (Abingdon)
Oratorios and Masses, Thrall (Squire Cooley)
The Practice of Sacred Music, Halter (Concordia)
They Sang a New Song, Mackay (Abingdon)
Music, Sacred and Profane, Routley
Church Music and Theology, Routley (Fortress)
O Sing Unto the Lord, Horn (Fortress)
The Singing Church, Liemohn (Augsburg)
Music in American Life (Chap. XV), Zanzig (Oxford U.)
Gilbert's Manual for Choir Loft and Pulpit, Gilbert (Scribner)
The Gift to Be Simple, Andrews (Dover Pub.)
Music in Evangelism, Kerr (Gospel Mus. Pb.)
Twentieth Century Church Music, Routley (Oxford U. Pr.)
Sacred Music, Robertson (Chanticleer Pr).
Song of the Church, Pierik (Longmans)

Christian Education

Use of Music in Christian Education, Morsch (Westminster Pr.)
Music in Christian Education, Thomas (Abingdon)
Music in the Religious Growth of Children, Shields (Abingdon)
Fundamentals of the Faith, Edit. by Henry (Zondervan)

General Church History

Christianity Through the Centuries, Cairns (Zondervan)

Appendix

Worship

Christian Worship, Hedley (Macmillan)
Christian Worship, Garrett (Augsburg)
A Guidebook to Worship Services of Sacred Music, Heaton (Bethany Press)
Music in Protestant Worship, Steere (John Knox)
Protestant Worship Music, Etherington (Holt, Rinehart, Winston)
Worship, Reed (Augsburg)

Adult Choirs

Building a Church Choir, Wilson and Lyall (Schmitt, Hall, McCreary)
Choirs and Choral Music, Mees (Scribners)
The Amateur Choir Director, Hjortsrang (Abingdon)
Handbook for Directors, Fuller and Atkinson (Pro Art)

Age-Group Choirs

Organizing and Directing Children's Choirs, Ingram (Abingdon)
Leading Children's Choirs, Sample (Broadman)
Youth Choirs, Miller (Flammer)
The Children's Choir Vol. I, Jacobs (Fortress)
The Children's Choir Vol. II, Tufts (Fortress)
Games and Songs of American Children, Newell (Dover)
A Guide for Youth Choirs, Ingram (Abingdon)

Hymnology

Hymnody of the Christian Church, Benson (Geo. H. Doran Co.)
Studies of Familiar Hymns, 1st Ed., Benson (Westminster)
Studies of Familiar Hymns, 2nd Ed., Benson (Westminster)
Hymns in Christian Worship, Jefferson (Rockliff: E. C. Schirmer)
Famous Stories of Inspiring Hymns, Emurian (W. A. Wilde)
Our Hymnody (Methodist) Hymn Stories, McCutcheon (Abingdon)
The Chorales, Their Origin and Influence, Wilson (Faith Pr., London)
101 Hymns in the Lives of Men, McCutcheon (Abingdon-Cokesbury)
The Hymn in History and Literature, Reeves (Century)
History and Use of Hymns and Hymn Tunes, Breed
Hymns of Worship and Service
Hymns of Our Faith, Reynolds (Broadman)
The Hymns of Methodism, Bett (Epworth Pr.)
Judson Concordance to Hymns, Judson (Judson)
Old Favorite Songs and Hymns, MacKenzie
A Hymn Is Born, Bonner (Broadman)
A Treasury of Hymns, Leiper and Simon (Simon & Schuster)
The English Hymn — Its Development and Use in Worship, Benson (John Knox)

Two Hundred Hymn Stories, Lorenz (Lorenz)
The Gospel in Hymns, Julian (Bailey)
The Story of Our Hymns, Haeussler (Eden)
The Story of the Church's Song, Millar (John Knox)
The Hymn and Congregational Singing, Sydnor (John Knox)
Hymn Tunes of Lowell Mason, Mason (Univ. Pr.)
Music in Worship, Ashton (Pilgrim)
*A Survey of Christian Hymnody, Reynolds (Holt, Rinehart, Winston)

Organ, Piano

*The Organist and Hymn Playing, Lovelace (Abingdon)
*The Pianist and Church Music, Mathis (Abingdon)
The Organist and Choirmaster, Etherington (Macmillan)
Playing a Church Organ, Conway (Literature Press, London)
Organ Stops and Their Artistic Registration, Audsley (Augsburg)
Basic Principles of Service Playing, Walter (Abingdon)
Dictionary of Pipe Organ Stops, Irwin (Schirmer)
Church Organ Accompaniment, Conway (Macmillan)
The Organ as a Musical Meduim, Fesperman (Coleman-Ross)
Organ Stops and Their Use, Whitworth (Pitmann)
An Introduction to the Technique of Palestrina, Andrews (Novello)
Effective Hymn Playing, Anderson (Augsburg)
Method of Organ Playing, Gleason (Appleton)

Church Music History

*History of American Church Music, Ellinwood (Morehouse-Gorham Co.)
*Music in the History of the Western Church, Dickinson (Scribner)
Church Music in History and Practice, Douglas (Scribner)
The History of Catholic Church Music, Fellerer (Helicon Press)
A History of Western Music, Grout (Norton)

Liturgy, Chants, Responses

*Manual of Plainsong, Briggs and Frere (Augsburg)
*Gregorian Chant, Apel (Bloomington, Indiana Pr.)
Book of Responses, Fuller (Pro. Art Pub.)
The Simplicity of Plainsong, Field (J. Fischer)

Music Buildings, Rooms, Equipment

*Music Buildings, Rooms (Bul. #17) (Music Educators National Conf., 1201 — 16th St., N.W., Wash. D.C.)
When You Build Your Church, Scotford (Meredith Pr.)

Specific, Occasional, Special

Christmas, Its Carols, Customs and Legends, Heller (Schmitt, Hall & McCreary)
Christmas Carols, Their Authors and Composers, Mottinger (G. Schirmer)
Treasury of Easter Music, Music for Passiontide, Reed (Emerson)
New Songs and Carols for Children (All year 'round), Grime (Carl Fischer)

Training and Techniques

Choral Conducting, Davison (Harvard Univ. Pr.)
Choral Technique and Interpretation, Coward (Gray)
Vocal Technique for Children and Youth, Ingram (Abingdon)
Popular Method of Sight Singing, Damrosch (G. Schirmer)
Choral Music and Its Practice, Cain (Witmark)
Basic Principles of Singing, Rice (Abingdon)
How to Lead Informal Singing, Hoffelt (Abingdon)
The Singer's Manual of English Diction, Marshall (G. Schirmer)

Signs, Symbols, Visual

Within the Chancel; Meaning and use of the chancel and its furnishings, signs, symbolism, church season, colors, etc., Stafford (Abingdon)
An Outline of Christian Symbolism, Wilson (Morehouse-Gorham)
Symbols of the Church, Whittemore (Whittemore)

INDEX

Abingdon Press 20
accompaniment,
 of hymns 95, 96
 organ 39, 162
 piano 95, 162
accompanist, 99
 duties 95
 qualifications 39
 uses 99
activities, social 66, 67
administration 19
adult choir 24
age-group choirs 68
agreements,
 verbal 30
 written 30
anthem 25
areas of representation 21
Asbury Methodist
 Church 106
attendance,
 rehearsal 50
 taking 74
 worship 50
baby-sitting 66
balance wheel 27
Barrie and Rockliff 89
bell choir 81
budgeting 170
car-pools 79
chants, Gregorian 84
choirs,
 adult 21, 61
 age-group 68
 attendance 50, 58
 dedication 49, 57, 183
 high school 73
 intermediate 79
 junior high school 78
 officers, duties of 62
 primary 81
 privileges 48
 probationary period 52
 requirements 48
 responsibilities 48, 59, 66
 sections 65
 volunteer 48
 warmup preparation 127
church school 22, 99
committee,
 music 19
 functions 20
 replacements 25
congregation,
 educating 95
 participation 83
 singing 83
contracts 30, 31
covenant, choir 53

creed 52
custodian 105
Decision 94
dedication,
 choir personnel 183
 music staff 28, 29
devotions, choir 48
director, music,
 experience 28
 qualifications 28
 technique 35
 training 28
 trial periods 29
discipline,
 choir membership 76
 self 49, 71
ensembles 152
equipment,
 cleaning and returning 108
 music room 142
ethics, 153
 breaches in 155
evangelizing agent 66, 68
facilities,
 music, improving 158
family participation 71
fellowship in choir 49
festivals and
 competitions, 110
 committees 110
future, planning for 172
Graham, Billy 94
Gregory, Pope 84
growth,
 professional 29, 43
 program 172
 spiritual 66, 185
high school choir 34
hiring,
 music director 28
 organist 39
hymn,
 accompanying 95
 adaptations 84, 92
 changes 89
 classic 94
 content 88
 "good old" and "new" 89
 gospel 94
 information on 97
 interpretation 94, 96
 melody of 91
 selection of 85
 tastes, improving 93
 teaching to
  congregation 94, 96
 texts 90
 theology of 90
hymn-of-the-month 98

hymns of,
 adoration 85
 confession 85
 dedication 85
 supplication 85
hymnals,
 changes in 88
 composition of 83, 92
 denominational 83
 primary, for 82
 subjects, extent of 86
instrumental,
 program 22, 152
 rehearsal room 133
 uses 152
integrity,
 personal 153, 155
 professional 153, 155
interest, year-round 181
introits 85
Jefferson, H. A. L. 89
Keach, Benjamin 88
lay personnel 20
leaders,
 choice of 21
 choir section 65
 song 101
liaison,
 pastor and director 20, 26
librarian,
 duties 64
 procedures 149
library, music,
 chairman 64
 equipment 160
 function 148
 procedures 149
 room 160
Lovelace, Austin C. 20
Luther, Martin 84
McMurry College 111
membership,
 chairman 63
 choir 49
 eligibility 66
men's classes 102
Meredith Press 94
minister (pastor) 19, 20, 22,
  26, 33, 52, 59, 85, 86, 94,
  128, 153, 157, 167, 170
minister of music (see
 "director of music")
ministry of music,
 current status 29
 record form 72
music,
 cataloguing 64
 choosing 26
 filing 64
 marking 64
 reading 103